Mitchell Symons wa[...] educated at Mill Hill School and the LSE, where he studied law. Since leaving BBC TV, where he was a researcher and then a director, he has worked as a writer, broadcaster and journalist. He was a principal writer of early editions of the board game Trivial Pursuit and has devised many television formats. He is also the author of more than thirty books, and currently writes a weekly column for the *Sunday Express*.

www.kidsatrandomhouse.co.uk

Also by Mitchell Symons:

HOW TO AVOID A WOMBAT'S BUM

Coming soon:

MITCHELL SYMONS

Why eating BOGEYS is good for you

. . . and other crazy facts explained!

RED FOX

WHY EATING BOGEYS IS GOOD FOR YOU
A RED FOX BOOK 978 1 862 30184 9

First published in Great Britain by Doubleday,
an imprint of Random House Children's Books
A Random House Group Company

Doubleday edition published 2007

Red Fox edition published 2008

5 7 9 10 8 6 4

The Random House Group Limited supports the Forest Stewardship Council (FSC), the leading international forest certification organization. All our titles that are printed on Greenpeace-approved FSC-certified paper carry the FSC logo. Our paper procurement policy can be found at www.rbooks.co.uk/environment.

Set in Optima

Red Fox Books are published by Random House Children's Books,
61–63 Uxbridge Road, London W5 5SA

www.**kidsatrandomhouse**.co.uk
www.**rbooks**.co.uk

Addresses for companies within The Random House Group Limited can be found at:
www.randomhouse.co.uk/offices.htm

THE RANDOM HOUSE GROUP Limited Reg. No. 954009

A CIP catalogue record for this book is available from the British Library.

Printed in the UK by CPI Bookmarque, Croydon, CR0 4TD.

To bogey-munchers everywhere

WHERE CAN I FIND QUESTIONS ABOUT . . . ?

Blame it on my father. He was a great bloke but he would always disagree with *anything* anyone said just for the fun of it. He would even argue about the weather, which, let's face it, is the one thing on which *everyone* always agrees.

Anyway, I've clearly inherited – along with his double chin – Dad's habit of looking at the flip side of just about everything. For some time now I've wanted to write a book that would answer the sort of questions you don't even find asked elsewhere, let alone answered.

That's because I really do need to know whether identical twins have identical fingerprints, why we don't wear seat belts on trains, whether you can actually lose weight by eating celery, whether it's possible to knock yourself out using your own fist, what happens to a cow if you don't milk it, why anyone would want to pop a weasel, what would happen to aeroplane passengers if someone opened the emergency exit while it was in the air and, yes, whether eating bogeys is bad for you.

But I haven't just been pondering my own queries; friends and readers of my columns in magazines and newspapers have asked me such posers as: *Do two wrongs make a right? Why is the sea blue? Is it cheaper to send yourself as a parcel to Australia rather than flying on an aeroplane?* and *Why did anyone even bother trying to put Humpty Dumpty back together again?*

So I would like to take this opportunity to thank all the extremely clever people who helped me – intentionally or inadvertently (and why don't we say 'advertently'?) – to answer these extraordinary questions.

Now for some even more important acknowledgements because, without these people, this book couldn't have been written at all: (in alphabetical order) Luigi Bonomi, Penny Chorlton, Annie Eaton, Emma Eldridge, Shannon Park, Mari Roberts and Doug Young.

In addition, I'd also like to thank the following people for their help, contributions and/or support: Gilly Adams, Jeremy Beadle, Marcus Berkmann, Paul Donnelley, Jonathan Fingerhut, Jenny Garrison, Philip Garrison, Kirsty MacArthur, Tricia Martin, William Mulcahy, Bryn Musson, Sophie Nelson, Nicholas Ridge, Charlie Symons, Jack Symons, Louise Symons, David Thomas, Martin Townsend, Rhys Willson and Rob Woolley. If I've missed anyone out, then please know that – as with any mistakes in the book – it's entirely down to my own stupidity.

Mitchell Symons, 2007
thatbook@mail.com

Is eating bogeys bad for you?

According to statistics, only 3 per cent of people eat their own bogeys. I say *only* because, if I'm honest, I've always eaten mine and I've often caught my sons having a quick nibble too. Are we really that unusual or, as I suspect, are most people just too embarrassed to own up?

Well, all that may change if an Austrian doctor named Dr Friedrich Bischinger has his way. He says that people who pick their noses are healthier, happier and probably better in tune with their bodies than people who don't.

At this point, I should mention that the main risk of picking your nose is not the dirt you might find there but the dirt you might introduce, which could subsequently enter your body. So, if you're going to pick your nose, make sure you do it with clean fingers.

Having issued a health warning, let me now return to Dr Bischinger, who says, 'With the finger you can get to places you just can't reach with a handkerchief, keeping your nose far cleaner. And eating the dry remains of what you pull out is a great way of strengthening the body's immune system. Medically, it makes great sense and is a perfectly natural thing to do. In terms of the immune system, the nose is a filter in which a great deal of bacteria is collected, and when this mixture arrives in the intestines, it works just like a medicine. I would recommend a new approach where children are *encouraged* to pick their nose. It is a completely natural response and medically a good idea as well.'

So there you have it: you *can* eat your own bogeys. But don't tell Mum and Dad I said so.

NB: However, you shouldn't eat your own earwax. This isn't good stuff.

How did Reading, Writing and Arithmetic come to be known as 'the three Rs', when only one begins with R?

Fair question – especially as you'd expect something to do with education to be correct. The dictionary defines the three Rs as an 'expression for reading, (w)riting, and (a)rithmetic – the fundamentals of an education'. In fact, it turns out to have been coined for real (but in error) by Sir William Curtis, an early-19th-century Lord Mayor of London, at the end of a speech in favour of elementary education. Sir William was bad at spelling, and genuinely thought all three words started with the letter R!

reading riting

rithmetic

Is it true that one human year equals seven dog years?

Sort of, but it's misleading, because there's no way that a 14-year-old dog is like a 98-year-old human. How many 98-year-olds do you know who can chase after balls and return sticks?

That's why dog experts have devised another way of equating human years with dog years. What they say is that the first dog year equals 21 human years, and every subsequent dog year equals just four human years.

This produces the following table:

DOG AGE	HUMAN EQUIVALENT
1	21
2	25
3	29
4	33
5	37
6	41
7	45
8	49
9	53
10	57
11	61
12	65
13	69
14	73

That looks more sensible, though I still don't know many 73-year-olds who can chase after balls and return sticks . . .

Rivers flow into the sea, so how come rivers are freshwater but the sea is saltwater?

I think about this question every time I take my boat down the river Arun into the sea: is there a point where the water goes from fresh to salty? If the harbour entrance were not so choppy (because of the sea hitting the walls) and there weren't so many people around, I'd like to take some samples and see for myself. Fortunately, thanks to geographer Joe Finlay, it isn't necessary.

'The sea is salty because for over three billion years it has taken salty minerals from the earth's crust. As a result, there is a huge quantity of salt left in the water – so much that if all the seas in the world dried up, the amount of salt left behind would be enough to build a wall of salt round the equator 150 miles high and one mile thick.'

OK, I've got that, but what about the river water flowing into it?

'The rivers are made up of rainwater, which is fresh, and river water only *becomes* salty once it flows into the sea. At the point where the river is closest to the sea – at the estuary – the water is more "brackish", or saltier. The important thing to remember is that rivers flow into seas – and not the other way round.'

In Monopoly, is it better to pay a £10 fine or take a Chance?

A game of Monopoly is my idea of a proper sporting contest – especially as I know all the tricks of the game. For example, three houses are better than a hotel, and the orange set is the best set on the board as the houses only cost £100 each and you trap people as they get out of jail.

You might be interested to know that, according to the statistics, the most-landed-upon squares on the board are (in order): Trafalgar Square, Go, Marylebone Station, Free Parking, Marlborough Street, Vine Street, King's Cross Station, Bow Street, Water Works and Fenchurch Street Station.

As for the question, with six 'nasty' cards out of 16 in the Chance deck, you are better off paying the fine. Especially if you have developed properties and the two street-repairs cards haven't been seen in a while.

But you if have no houses or hotels, you would be a bit of a wuss to pay a tenner – especially as your opponent can be guaranteed to make chicken noises and/or to show you the Chance card you would have got, which is invariably 'Advance to Go'.

How and when did the American accent evolve?

I thought maybe the American accent evolved from the West Country accent (for example, the Plymouth Brethren who went across on the *Mayflower* to colonize America). Then I asked linguist Dr Karen Landy, and her reply startled me.

'It's not so much that their accent evolved, but that

ours did. *We* were the ones who changed, not them. Let me give you an example. One sound we associate with American English is a distinctive growl produced near the back of the mouth on a word ending in R. This sound is standard in the west of England (Shakespeare would have growled his final R sounds), in the north and in Ireland. In the 19th century most of the settlement in North America from our islands came from the north and west of England and from Ireland (especially the six northern counties of Ulster).'

She paused for breath, which gave me a chance to ask her about the accents of the other immigrants.

'The German and Irish accents have definitely had an impact on the American accent. Also the US rejected British dominance early on in its history. That meant rejecting British teachers and administrators, for example, which meant reduced exposure to the accent of Britain. But really, what's puzzling is that after all this time and such different histories, our accents are still so alike.'

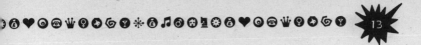

Why do we have tonsils?

The human body is constantly evolving but it takes a long time. As a result, we still have bits and pieces we don't really need any more – like the appendix, which is the remains of an additional digestive system that helped us to absorb the vegetables that used to make up most of the human diet. Tonsils fall into a similar category – although they do still serve a purpose by helping to stop germs from entering our bodies through our mouths. However, as anyone who's suffered tonsillitis will confirm, tonsils are more bother than they are worth.

Why don't we have to wear seat belts on trains?

We couldn't wear seat belts on trains even if we wanted to – because there aren't any!

Unlike cars, which tend to impact head-on in a crash, a train is most likely to be derailed and roll over on its side, so a seat belt on a train wouldn't make any difference whatsoever to the passengers' safety.

Add to that the fact that trains very rarely crash (more people die on the roads in a single day than on trains in a whole year) and you can see that it would be unpopular with passengers and expensive for the train operators.

But why do we wear seat belts on aeroplanes? Seat belts on aeroplanes are not fitted in the event of a crash, but for safety during the movement caused by take-off and landing and turbulence. At these times, the seat belts stop people from being thrown around the aircraft. Trains, on the other hand, run on fixed rails and don't have those severe movement problems.

Why do we have an April Fool's Day?

Most cultures – ancient and modern – have a special day when playing practical jokes is encouraged. This day often occurs at the same time as the arrival of spring, when everyone is relieved to have survived winter and is looking forward to summer.

That's the background, but the reason the date is 1 April might be because a few hundred years ago New Year's Day was celebrated on 25 March, with festivities that ended on 1 April. When the calendar was changed (from the Julian to today's Gregorian calendar, for those who would like to know), and New Year's Day became 1 January, the people who still celebrated it on 1 April were called April Fools.

Celery has no calories, so can eating it make you lose weight?

First of all, is it true that celery has no calories? I mean, even if it's mostly water, it must have *some* calorie content – otherwise it wouldn't exist. So I bought a packet of celery – never let it be said that I don't do any research. And, no, it is *not* calorie-free. On the packet it says precisely how many calories it has: 7 per 100 grams.

So the question is this: does chewing 100 grams of celery consume more than 7 calories?

In the absence of any other volunteers, I decided to experiment on myself. I sat down with my 500-gram pack of celery and worked my way through it.

All right, I cheated by throwing away the tough part at the bottom and the grassy stuff on the top, and I spat out the stringy bits, but I must have consumed about 400 grams in half an hour.

Given that 100 grams is 7 calories, this means that I consumed 28 calories.

But how many calories did I use up eating it?

Hard to tell, but here are some comparisons. In 30 minutes, you use up 75 calories just having a bath, or 165 calories doing some chores around the house, so you're going to use up more than 28 calories eating celery. But you'll also use up 72 calories just watching TV, so who needs to chew celery anyway? The point is, what else might you – or, rather, I – have been doing in that half-hour? And almost anything else would have used up more calories.

Everyone knows that *Blue Peter* is a brilliant TV programme, but how did it get its name?

Traditionally, when ships were ready to set sail from ports, they would hoist a blue-and-white flag called the Blue Peter. When John Hunter Blair, the programme's creator, was trying to come up with a name, he chose this because he saw the programme as a voyage of adventure and discovery for its viewers.

And, as several generations of British children can confirm, wasn't he proved right?

According to the Sunday newspapers, you can buy a plot of land on the moon. So who would you apply to for permission if you wanted to build on it?

If you think this is an extraordinary question, you will be amazed by the answer. In the 1960s, when space travel proved to be possible, the Americans and the Russians (who were competing to get to the moon first) agreed on just one thing: that no one country should own the moon. In 1967 they signed an Outer Space Treaty. However, an American named Dennis M. Hope saw a loophole. While no *country* could own the moon, there was nothing to stop an individual doing so. On 22 November 1980 he filed a declaration of ownership.

Call him a lunatic if you will, but he's a rich one. And a diligent one. He duly divided the lit surface of the moon into individual square acres. He also did a deal with the US Navy for its satellite to photograph it so that he would be able to provide his customers with photographic 'proof' of their landholding.

He called his business the Lunar Embassy and there are 'ambassadors' throughout the world. Britain's Lunar Ambassador is Francis Williams who, through Moon Estates, will 'sell' you a unique acre of the moon – with a deed, constitution, property map and mineral rights, all for £16.75.

Developing your land is trickier. I checked with a lawyer and when he could stop giggling he told me that planning would be difficult.

'Even supposing that they have perfect entitlement' – Dennis Hope is certain that they do – 'against anyone else on Earth, what about people from other galaxies? Meanwhile, there are no planning regulations in place. There is no authority to give you the permission you need to build whatever you want.'

Is it possible – as people say it is – to fit the entire population of the world on to the Isle of Wight?

Actuaries are people who work for insurance companies, calculating the odds against various things occurring. My friend William Mulcahy is a top actuary, and when I asked him, he told me that 'At the moment, there are 6,406,230,000 people on the planet – 30 per cent of whom are under the age of 15. That means 4,484,361,000 adults and 1,921,869,000 children. Assuming that an *average* adult can stand on a rectangle of 0.2 square metres and an *average* child can stand on a rectangle of 0.1 square metres, we can say that adults require 896,872,200 square metres and children require 192,186,900 square metres. The total area needed is therefore 1,089,059,100 square metres or 1,089 square kilometres. Sadly, the Isle of Wight is 381 square kilometres. Therefore we can conclude that it is impossible to fit the world's population onto the Isle of Wight.'

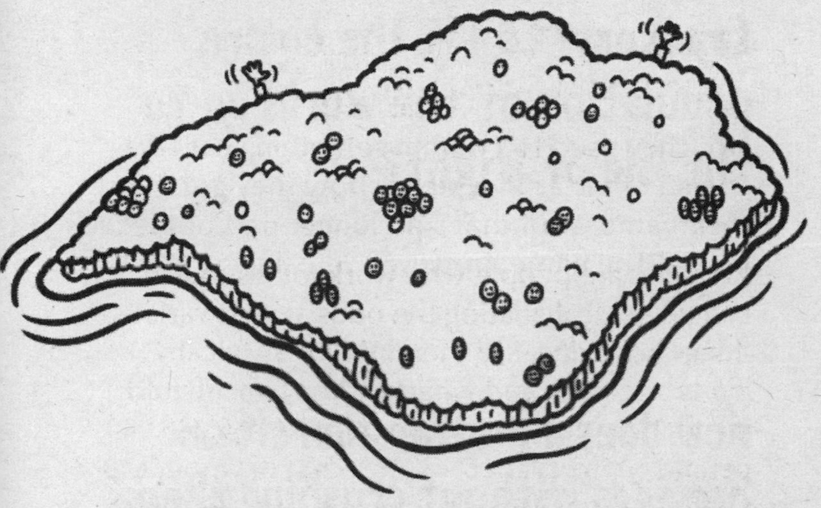

So why does everyone say you can fit the world's population onto the Isle of Wight?

'People like to create images to help them understand things. So imagining the population of the whole world in one spot gives us an idea of how many people there are altogether. And there must have been a time when it was possible to fit the whole world's population onto the Isle of Wight, but it was probably 200 years ago.'

Is there any cream in Cream Crackers?

No. They used to contain something called 'cream of tartar' – which is how they got their name – but that's no longer part of the recipe. The name, however, remains.

How does a mother hen sit on her eggs without crushing them?

The simple answer is that eggs are tougher than you think, while hens are softer than you think. Eggs are designed (by nature/evolution) to withstand this process.

My wife keeps hens that produce the most wonderful eggs and she (my wife, not the chicken) tells me that to make really good strong eggshells, hens need to eat lots of grit – which is why scratching around in the dirt is so good for them. And broody hens should be given soft straw bedding in which to sit on their eggs.

Why don't we eat squirrels?

My idea of frontier spirit is barbecuing a hamburger instead of frying it, so I haven't got a clue, but my mate Rob has lived, survived and thrived all over the world.

Rob explained: 'Squirrels are tree-rats with good PR [public relations]. We don't eat them because we don't want to catch rabies or any of the other horrible diseases they have – and sometimes transmit merely by skin contact. But that only applies to urban or suburban squirrels. Country squirrels are fine – so long as you catch one yourself and don't pick up a dead one. Once you've killed it, you skin it as though you were peeling an orange, removing the head and feet. Then you take out the internal organs and make sure – and this is very important – that you wash the animal thoroughly with water and vinegar. Then you simply cook it as though it was a chicken joint.'

What, using a jar of Chicken Tonight?

'Not advised.'

Why, because they're squirrels?

'No, because they're food.'

Is it true that goldfish have a memory span of only three seconds?

You could easily say no, the evidence being that they know when it is feeding time – which suggests they can remember for 24 hours at least. However, when I phoned a marine biologist to confirm this, he said that fish responding to knocks on the tank or even to feeding signals weren't displaying memory but instinct. As far as he was concerned, fish didn't have memories at all – at least not as we understand it. Which probably explains why they don't send each other birthday cards.

What's the difference between Holland and the Netherlands?

The two names are used interchangeably for the country that has The Hague as its capital, but they are not the same thing.

The Netherlands – which literally means 'low countries' – is short for the Kingdom of the Netherlands, which has 12 provinces.

Two of those provinces – North and South Holland – came to represent the whole country.

So if you're referring to the whole country, then you should use the Netherlands – otherwise it would be like calling the United Kingdom 'the Midlands'.

Is it really necessary to wait for food to be digested before swimming?

My mother used to make me wait for two hours after eating before I could go swimming. But it's not necessary – unless you've eaten a lot of carbohydrates (bread, potatoes, pasta, etc.), which might make you tired and sleepy. Look at Channel swimmers like David Walliams, who not only swim after eating, but eat *while* they are swimming!

Of course, you are probably not swimming the Channel, which requires special training. However, if you want to jump in the pool or splash around in the sea, there is no need to wait for ages after eating.

Why do people touch wood for luck?

Like so many superstitions and celebrations, this one has its origins in pagan times when people worshipped trees – especially oak trees – and touched them for luck (or knocked them to drive out evil spirits).

Later, after the life and death of Jesus Christ, people would touch wood for luck because Jesus' cross was made of wood.

Nowadays, many of us – whether we are Christians or not – touch wood routinely when we are hoping for something to happen or not to happen.

Why can't you tickle yourself?

Obviously, like anyone else, I'm aware that I can't tickle myself – or, indeed, scratch my own back with any great deal of pleasure. But why? I asked Dr Roland Powell, a medical doctor, to explain.

'I guess the basic reason why you can't tickle yourself – and get the same response as if another person were doing it to you – is because you can't introduce the element of surprise.

'And the reason that surprise is so important is because for a tickle to work, it requires your brain to be baffled. The sensations you experience in a tickle include pleasure and, because you don't know what's going to happen next, just a teensy bit of anxiety. If you tickle yourself, you are, of course, forewarned by your brain and your body's own inner sensory devices, which keep all parts of the body informed about what other parts of the body are doing. So you simply can't fool yourself.'

But why do we laugh when we're tickled?

'Good question. Your nervous system is conditioned to be scared of attack – this is a very primitive reflex. When you're tickled, there is a tension between this primitive reflex and your rational mind, which produces laughter.'

Kangaroos keep their babies in their pouches, so what happens to all the baby's poo?

According to zoologist Linda Vine, 'Kangaroos use their front feet to open up their pouches so that they can stick their heads in and lick their pouches clean.'

So they're licking out all the, er, droppings?

'Yes, that's right. Joeys – baby kangaroos – stay in the pouch for several months so their mothers have to clean around them. But even after they leave, they return when they are hungry, until either they can't squeeze in any longer or the mother kicks them out. In those circumstances, the mothers wait until they've left the pouch – temporarily or permanently – and then clean it out.'

Is the 'Oz' in *The Wizard of Oz* anything to do with Australia?

No! The author of the book – Frank L. Baum – was struggling to come up with a name when he found himself looking at his filing cabinet, where he saw A–N and O–Z. So I guess it was a straight choice between *The Wizard of An* and *The Wizard of Oz* . . . and we all know which one won.

Do royals really have blue blood?

No, they don't. It's red, just like yours and mine. Well, mine anyway – I can't speak for you. You might be an alien.

So why do people talk about the royals being blue-blooded?

According to the historian Dr Michael Morgan, it all goes back to 15th-century Spain where, he tells me, 'The royals were blond and fair-skinned and were keen to demonstrate the differences between themselves and the Moors who had invaded from Africa. So they said that not only was their skin fairer but their veins were also bluer – as a result of the "blue blood" running through them. From there, we got the idea that royal blood was blue.'

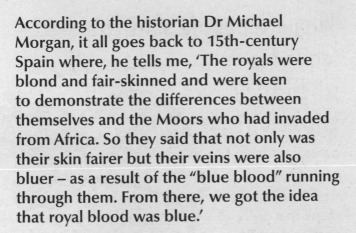

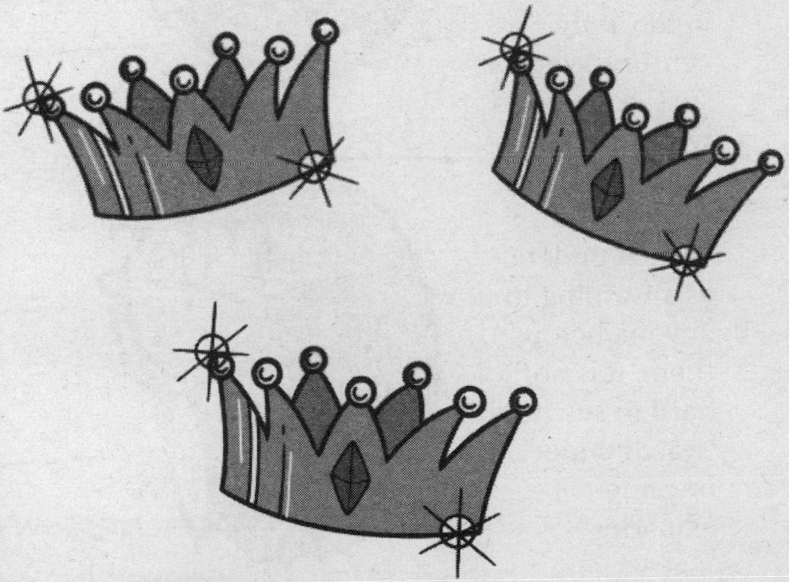

Why are people said to 'chunder' when they throw up?

This comes from the convict ships that were sent to Australia in the 19th century. When seasick convicts were about to throw up, they would shout, 'Watch under!' as a warning to anyone below them. It is not hard to see how 'watch under' became 'chunder'.

Why do you have to mount horses from the left side?

It's true, you know, you do have to. And yet it shouldn't matter which side you mount – or, in my case, clamber up – as a horse is, of course, symmetrical.

'There are two things to consider here,' said my wife, Penny, who has a lovely horse named Rosie: 'the historical and the practical. The reason why horses were originally mounted from the left was because men were carrying swords and, being right-handed, wore these swords on their left side [try to visualize it]. If they had mounted their horses on the right side, the swords would have got in the way and the horse might have been hurt.'

OK, I understand the history, but we don't carry swords any more. Mobile phones, yes, but swords never. So why can't we get on a horse from either side now?

'You can – so long as it's the side from which the horse is used to being mounted. But now we get to a practical consideration. As you know, horses get scared very easily. If a horse is used to being mounted from its left side, then it might "spook" if you mounted it from the right. That's why the custom of mounting from the left side has persisted: so that riders and horses alike can be confident that it is the correct side – the side with which the horse feels safe and comfortable.'

Does pushing the button repeatedly at pedestrian crossings make the lights change quicker?

There's no mystery to why we keep pushing these (and lift) buttons: even if it doesn't work, it gives us a feeling of control – just like when, as a kid, I used to count to a hundred while I was waiting for a bus.

Still, who knows? Well, the woman at my local council's traffic department seemed to.

'It depends,' she said. 'If the button hasn't already been pushed, yes, it does speed things up. But if the lights have recently changed, then pressing, or pushing repeatedly, will have no effect.'

OK.

But she wasn't finished. 'There are two ways pedestrian crossings respond to the control lights. On pelicon [PEdestrain LIght CONtrolled] crossings, pressing does have an effect, but there is a time delay if they have only just been on red – for obvious reasons. At complex junctions and traffic lights, the delay is usually already set, and using the button makes very little difference. But sometimes the lights will change *only* if the button is pressed, such as on busy main roads where few pedestrians would want to cross.'

Thanks.

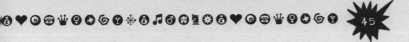

Why is something good described as the 'bee's knees' and not the ant's or the wasp's knees?

The expression 'the bee's knees' – meaning the very best – first became popular in the United States in the 1920s and it has nothing to do with bees, or any other insect.

There are two possible sources. It might come from the expression 'the BEs and Es', which itself was a short form of the phrase 'the be-alls and end-alls'.

The second possibility, and the one I prefer, is that it comes from 'the business', pronounced 'beeznees'.

Why are the numbers on a dartboard arranged the way they are?

The dartboard was created by Brian Gamlin, a carpenter from Bury in Lancashire, in 1896. He wanted the higher numbers, 18, 19 and 20, to be bracketed by the lower numbers (1 & 4, 3 & 7 and 1 & 5), and he wanted a good mix over the board. Because gravity makes a dart fall, he made the top of the dartboard 20 and one of the lower numbers, 3, at the bottom.

Much later *Darts World* magazine invited readers to come up with a different system, but no one improved on Mr Gamlin's version. This was made the official standard only in the 1970s. There are variations on this numbering pattern – such as in funfairs, where you have to score under 20 with three darts and every number on the board is 25.

Why don't cats wag their tails when they are happy, like dogs do?

Although we bracket cats and dogs together – they are both popular household pets – the animals are totally different from one another.

Dogs are pack animals. They need to convey their emotions to other members of the pack. (When dogs live with us human beings, we are the members of their pack.) One of the ways they convey their emotions is by wagging their tails to show pleasure.

Cats, on the other hand, are loners and have no need to convey anything – unless they want food. Instead they use their tails as part of a complex system of movement and balance, especially when they are stalking their prey.

Could chickens ever fly? If so, when did they lose the ability?

As I look out of my window into the garden, I can see a group (a herd? a pride? a kiev?) of chickens running around. Actually 'waddling' is a better word, because they are so fat.

I know nothing about these creatures but Penny, my wife and their keeper, is an expert. According to her, chickens *can* fly.

'All chickens have wings and most can fly, hence the expression "to fly the coop". But they weigh so much compared to their wingspan that they can't fly very high or far. This is why we can let them run loose in the garden during the day. However, their limited ability to fly does help them to escape their natural enemy, the fox. But with some chickens – like the one we call Houdini – you have to trim one or both of their wings so they can escape from a predator, but can't escape from the garden.'

What's the best thing to take for travel sickness?

We get travel sickness from the disturbance of the delicate balance in our inner ears. So what can we do to stop feeling sick?

On a car journey, it helps to keep looking outside the car so that the road's twists and turns are not so much of a shock to your system. For the same reason, it's probably best not to read or to play computer games.

Similarly, on a boat or a ship (the difference between the two being that you can put a boat on a ship but you cannot put a ship on a boat) it's better to get out on deck – if you're allowed to – than to stay below feeling grotty.

Window seats on planes can also help.

But what if that doesn't do the trick? Is there any other solution?

Well, there are pills you can take, but some of them leave you feeling sleepy even after the journey has finished. Some people wear special elasticated wristbands with studs that work on pressure points to stop nausea.

I suffer from travel sickness, and do you know what I find works better than anything? Ginger. It is natural and it has been proven to stop any form of travel sickness. You can get ginger tablets, but it is much easier – and nicer – to eat crystallized ginger. It works for me and I hope it works for you too!

What happens to a cow if you don't milk it?

If I'm honest, I wanted to hear that there would be a great explosion and the surrounding countryside would be covered in bits of cow. Sadly, the truth is a little less exciting. According to dairy farmer Clive Wilson, 'If you don't milk a cow, pressure builds up which simply stops the cow producing any more milk. Any milk still in her udder would be taken up by her body. This is what happens naturally when a calf stops feeding. But when you've got a high-yielding dairy cow, she's going to need milking or she'll be in a lot of pain and might contract an infection.'

How dangerous is that?

'Could be fatal.'

And might the cow explode?

'No, don't be silly.'

Why is it that if someone tells you there are a billion stars in the universe, you believe them, but if they tell you that paint is wet, you have to touch it to be sure?

I asked a philosopher friend of mine, who told me this: 'Most of us have an instinct for empirical (that is, provable) truths. You can't count the stars to confirm the number but you can touch the paint to check that it's wet. It's about control. However, there is another factor. It's called the "polymorphous perverse", where you do the exact thing you have been told not to do.'

Is this 'polymorphous perverse' thingy the same instinct that causes me to touch the plate just after a waiter says, 'Don't touch the plate – it's extremely hot'?

'Yes, it's the same thing.'

What's the best thing to do in a plummeting lift?

Pray. According to Dr Adrian Newman, a physicist, 'Assuming all the lift cables have gone, and assuming that the lift is falling at a speed of, say, 60 feet per second – or 40 miles per hour – there's nothing you can do to soften the impact. More to the point, at that sort of speed over that sort of distance, you are not going to get the time to think, let alone act. You're going to end up like a pancake.'

Is that it? What about jumping?

'Why?'

To minimize impact.

'Even if you had time to think, this would not be a good idea. You're travelling down at 40 miles per hour; how fast are you going to jump up – always assuming that you can time your jump just right? Four miles per hour? Five miles per hour? At best, you are still

travelling down at 40 minus 5 – at 35 miles per hour. You are still going to get splattered. Put it another way. Let's say you have a terminal velocity of 30 metres per second. Even if you were an Olympic athlete, you are only going to be able to leap up at a speed of 3 metres per second. So you are reducing your terminal velocity to 27 metres per second. It's like jumping from the 20th floor instead of the 22nd.'

Is there anything I can do? What about bracing myself or clinging to the sides?

'That's fine at slow speeds like five or ten miles per hour, and bending your knees will stop them being shoved up into your body, but in a plummeting lift that's useless. The best thing is to make sure that you only travel in lifts with very fat people so that if it does crash, there's a chance that they will cushion your fall!'

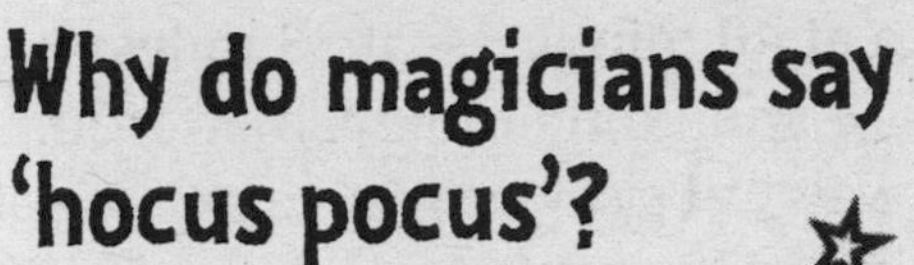

Why do magicians say 'hocus pocus'?

It is thought that the word 'hocus' comes from the word 'hoax' (after all, a trick is a kind of hoax) and that the word 'pocus' was added as an incantation that a magician would use as part of his act. The 17th-century magician who popularized the expression liked it so much he changed his name to . . . Hocus Pocus!

Is it cheaper to send yourself as a parcel to Australia rather than flying on an aeroplane?

Let's assume for a second that it was possible (which of course it isn't), and let's ignore the intense discomfort of travelling Down Under tied up in brown paper and string – how about the price? Actually, it would be more expensive. Let's say we're talking about a man who weighs 80 kilograms or about 12½ stone (which rules me out of making the trip). Air Mail costs £19.59 for a maximum 2 kilograms. Multiply that by 40 (to get to 80 kg) and you get £783.60. This compares unfavourably to the best discount air fares to Australia (£599 including two free stopovers). Surface Mail costs £8.62 for a maximum 2 kg. Again, multiply that by 40 and that comes to £344.80, which *sounds* cheaper but is of course just one way and the £599 quoted above is for a return ticket.

The above two methods are purely hypothetical (even ignoring the discomfort, etc.) because they only accept parcels up to 2 kg. There is another possibility – so long as you only weigh 30 kg the maximum weight that Parcel Force will send. This costs £247.50 (if you can make the weight) by air or £192 at the International Standard rate, but this latter option can take up to 30 days. And you won't get any food or in-flight entertainment.

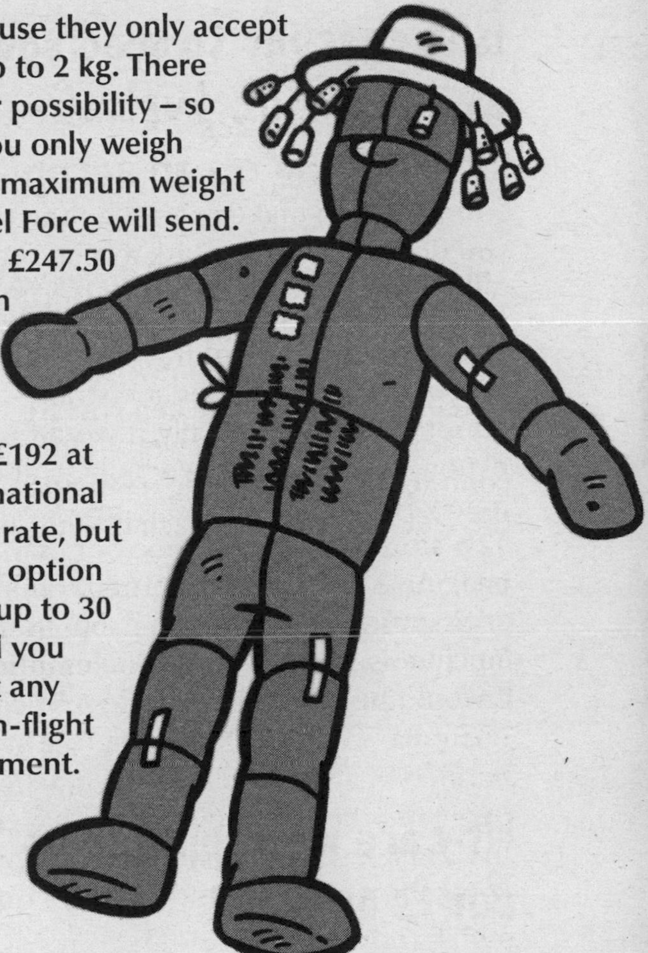

Why does my stomach rumble when I'm hungry?

Your stomach makes noises all the time. If you don't believe me, ask a friend to listen to it by putting their ear against it. The thing is, when you're not hungry, you don't hear your thick, strong stomach muscles continually squeezing. However, when you *are* hungry, the noise of that squeezing – alternately contracting and relaxing – is made louder by the fact that your stomach is empty.

Imagine a drum. If you stuffed it full of rags or tissues, you wouldn't be able to make much noise with it, but if you emptied it first, it would be a lot louder.

Why are we supposed to 'mind our Ps and Qs'?

The most popular explanation for this is that the Ps and Qs represent 'Pleases' and 'thankQs'.

However, this explanation became popular after the expression was already in use, and no one knows the real story. There are three possibilities:

1. That it comes from the printing industry: when old-fashioned typesetters assembled letters for printing, they were looking at the letters from the back, which means that 'p' and 'q' could be mistaken for each other.

OR

2. That innkeepers would run tabs for regular customers, with Ps representing pints and Qs quarts. If customers didn't want to be cheated when it came to settling up, they had to 'mind their Ps and Qs'.

OR

3. That dancing instructors – using fashionable French – would warn their pupils to mind their *pieds* (feet) and *perruques* (wigs).

I offer you all three so you can choose for yourself!

What's the origin of the expression 'in a nutshell'?

You know when you're talking to someone and, eventually, you decide to summarize your point in a few words, you might say, 'In a nutshell, what I'm saying is . . .'? Well, that's all thanks to an Englishman named Peter Bales, who made a tiny Bible that was small enough to fit into a walnut shell. From that, we get the expression 'in a nutshell' to cover any example of a short argument or point.

Is it dangerous to crack your fingers?

According to Dr Roland Powell, it is not dangerous. 'I think that most people who do it are double-jointed and what they're doing is snapping the ligaments in the fingers over the joint's surface.'

But I thought that there was a ball of fluid or something that was responsible for the noise?

'There's fluid in the joint but only a minimal amount and that isn't what makes the noise: it's the snapping of the ligament.'

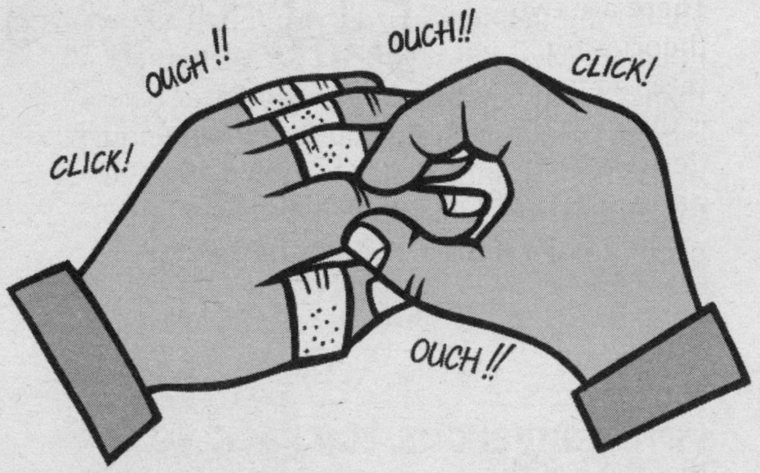

So finger-snappers can carry on to their hearts' content?

'No.'

Why not? You said it wasn't dangerous.

'Maybe not, but it is very annoying.'

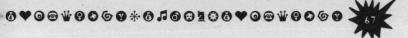

Why are British people called 'Poms' or 'Pommies'?

There are two theories for this: the first is that pom is derived from pomegranate – a sort of rhyming slang for 'immigrant'. The other explanation is that the British convict settlers had the letters POHM (Prisoners of His Majesty) stamped all over their clothes.

There's an MI5 and an MI6, but is there an MI1, MI2, MI3 and MI4?

According to my intelligence source, MI1 was Military Intelligence Administration; MI2 was Military Intelligence for the Middle East, China, Burma and Tibet; MI3 was Military Intelligence for Western Europe, the USA and South America; and MI4 was the section dealing with maps and surveys.

During the 1960s all these sections were gathered together under the umbrella of the Defence Intelligence Staff.

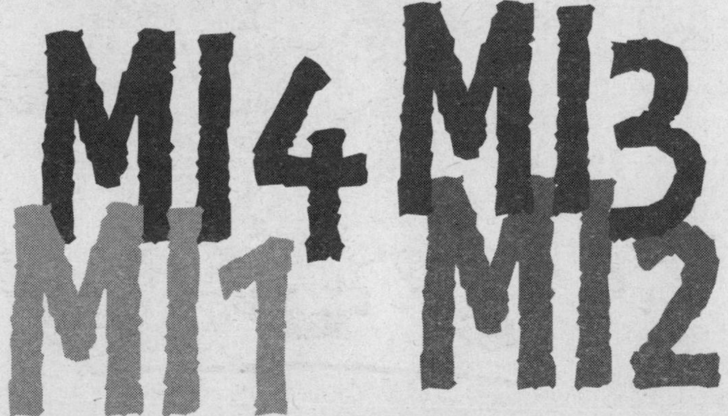

Why does a man's bicycle have a crossbar?

According to Raleigh, Britain's biggest bicycle manufacturer: 'The question should be, "Why *don't* women's bicycles have crossbars?"

Men's bicycles have crossbars because the triangular construction is the most efficient type of geometry for a stable frame.'

The reason why women's bicycles don't have crossbars is historical: the long skirts and petticoats once worn by women meant that crossbars got in the way, and it was more elegant for a woman to step through the frame than to lift her leg over it. Having said that, these days any serious female cyclist buying a mountain bike or road-race cycle will choose one made with a man's frame.

In the nursery rhyme, why did anyone even bother to try to put Humpty Dumpty back together again?

Like many nursery rhymes, this one was based on real life. Far from being an egg, Humpty Dumpty was King Richard III, whose appearance earned him that nickname. After the Battle of Bosworth Field in 1485, no one could help poor old Humpty back on the wall – or throne – again.

We drink the milk of cows, goats and sheep, so why does no one drink pig's milk?

I asked my friendly farmer, Clive Wilson, for the answer to this.

'If you wanted to drink pig's milk, there would be nothing to stop you – if you could get it. That's the problem, though: getting it. You see, a cow has one or two calves and makes her milk available whenever they want it. A pig, on the other hand, has several piglets and, so that they all get fed, she has to make sure they all suckle together. The way she does this is by only giving up her milk when all her teats are being sucked. In order for us, as farmers, to get milk from a pig, we would have to make sure that all the teats were being milked simultaneously, and even then we'd be lucky if we got any for more than a couple of seconds.'

Why do we have eyebrows?

Why indeed? They don't really *do* anything.

When I looked into this some more, I discovered I was wrong. Eyebrows are important! They do lots of things. They stop sweat and dandruff from getting into the eyes, and they even trap 'foreign objects' – anything from tiny wood splinters to insects or even dust – before they can fall into the eyes.

But that's not all! We also use our eyebrows to show our feelings. We raise one or both of them to show when we're surprised or amused and we close them together when we're cross or confused.

Useful things, eyebrows.

Why are there no fat insects?

Can't say I've ever stopped to think about this one. But now you mention it . . .

So I phoned my pal Lucy, who used to work at the Natural History Museum, and she told me that insects have their skeletons on the outside, so they simply can't get fat. What a brilliant idea, I said, thinking of the possibilities for fatties like me, but she pointed out that this doesn't mean they can overeat. Having their skeletons on the outside means that if they scoff too much, they explode.

Is there any connection between toast – as in grilled bread – and the toast we propose when we drink?

Yes, there is. In ancient Rome they used to put pieces of burned bread (i.e. toast) into their wine glasses because the charcoal helped to reduce the wine's acidity. From toast to toasting was but a small step.

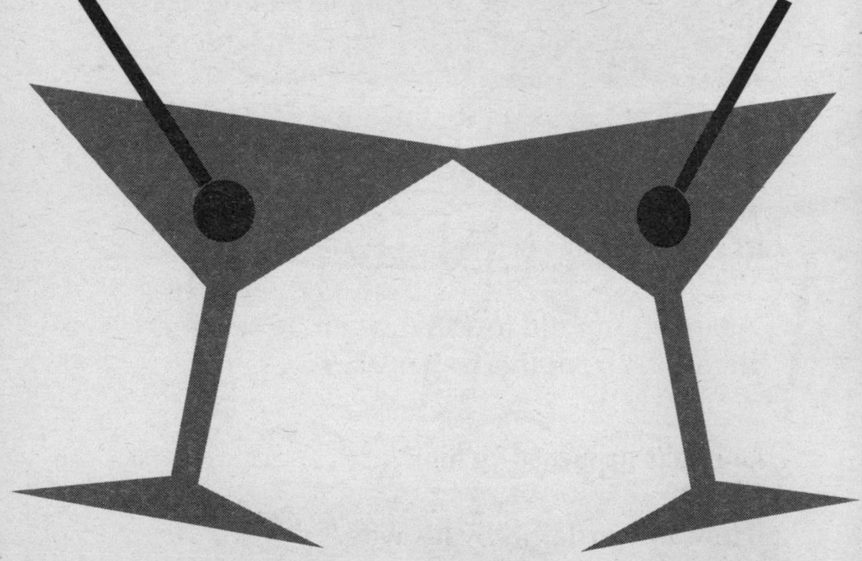

Why are VIPs given the red carpet?

I turned to social anthropologist (someone who studies the social and cultural development of human beings) Dr Lorraine Mackintosh for the answer to this.

She did some research, and then told me: 'Red dye was always used for carpets for important people because it was so expensive to produce and was therefore a mark of respect. If we go back far enough, to ancient Greece, red was the colour of the gods because it symbolized blood, and only the gods – or the priests – could walk on red carpets.'

What if someone broke that rule?

'Agamemnon did just that when he returned victorious from the Trojan Wars.'

And what happened to him?

'He was murdered by his wife.'

Could a coin dropped from the top of a skyscraper kill someone?

'Not that old chestnut,' said physicist Dr Adrian Newman when I phoned him. 'No, it wouldn't.'

Could you expand on that?

'All right,' he said: 'no, it *definitely* wouldn't. How's that? Listen, I've just got in. I'll phone you back when I've had something to eat.'

An hour later he called me back and apologized for having been grumpy. Then he said: 'Now, this coin business. OK, let's say you threw it from the Eiffel Tower, it would reach its terminal velocity after about 300 metres—'

Which is the height of the Eiffel Tower.

'If you say so. Anyway, at this point it would be travelling at around 175 miles per hour.

So, yes, it would give someone a headache – it might even fracture their skull – but it wouldn't kill them.'

Are you sure?

'Sure I'm sure. 175 miles per hour is a lot slower than a bullet, and besides, coins aren't shaped like bullets.'

What about a higher building, like the Empire State Building?

'No, in many ways that's safer. In fact, it's possible that a coin dropped from the top of the building would not even reach the street. Because of wind variations and up-draughts, the coin would hit the side and be caught in one of the building's nooks and crannies. Sorry to disappoint you.'

On whom – or on what – was the nursery rhyme character Little Jack Horner based?

Little Jack Horner
Sat in the corner
Eating a Christmas pie.
He put in his thumb
And pulled out a plum
And said, 'What a good boy am I!'

Like many of our nursery rhymes, this one dates from the 16th century. Cast your minds back to the time when King Henry VIII was confiscating large chunks of church land. Richard Whiting, the abbot of the richest abbey in England, wanted to gain favour with the king and so he sent him a Christmas pie with the title deeds to 12 manor houses baked inside it. However, Whiting's crafty steward, Jack Horner, stole the deed to the manor of Mells, a real 'plum' of an estate, and kept it for himself. Hence the nursery rhyme.

At least, that's the story . . .

Instead of being very rude and swearing, some people say 'Gordon Bennett'. Did he exist and, if so, who was he?

James Gordon Bennett (1841–1918) was an American newspaper proprietor who was so wealthy and enjoyed such a lavish lifestyle that his name became an exclamation.

- During his lifetime he spent $40 million.
- He once gave a train porter a tip of $14,000.
- He once burned a wad of thousands of francs because all the notes in his pocket were causing him discomfort.
- He built a yacht – the *Lysistrata* – which had a padded room for housing a cow to provide him with fresh milk.
- In 1877 he got drunk at a party at his fiancée's house and mistook the fireplace for a toilet. His fiancée's brother challenged him to a duel (neither man was hurt), but he fled to Paris.

- In Paris his favourite hobby was smashing up restaurants (and he wasn't even a rock star) – although he always paid for the damage.

- He once went to a restaurant in Monte Carlo and found that it was full, so he bought the restaurant and instructed the head waiter that he was always to reserve a table for him.

All together now: 'Gordon Bennett!'

Why is the question mark the shape it is?

According to Dr Karen Landy, punctuation is a relatively recent invention. 'Ancient Western and Middle Eastern languages didn't use any punctuation. All the words just ran into one another. The Assyrians and the Babylonians put a space at the end of each sentence but that was all they did for punctuation.'

So when did punctuation start?

'In about AD 600. One theory is that it came about because of the Church. St Augustine

was worried that priests pausing in the wrong place might convey the wrong message to their congregations, and so he ordered dots and squiggles to be inserted into manuscripts.'

Thanks for the lesson, Dr L., but what about the ??

'I'm coming to that,' she said coldly. 'At the start of the 9th century, Charlemagne's court standardized punctuation. The first form of the question mark was a full stop with a tilde (~) over it. This, of course, evolved into the familiar question-mark shape. Then the arrival of the printing press meant that the standardized punctuation became widely used and accepted.'

Why don't women have beards?

I phoned my pet trichologist to ask him the reason why.

'It's all to do with women's hormones, which stimulate the growth of hair on the head but stunt the growth of facial and body hair. It doesn't *always* work, but then that's where hair-removal creams come in. The key difference between what you would call "the sexes" but what I would call "the genders" comes at adolescence. So while the male sex hormone kicks in to stimulate the growth of the beard and body hair, in females it works to stop it. A similar thing happens – in reverse – with head hair later in the life cycle: men lose theirs while women (usually) maintain theirs.'

But why?

'Why?'

Why don't women have beards? You've explained that they don't but you haven't said *why*.

'You'd better speak to an anthropologist.'

So I phoned Dr Lorraine Mackintosh, who told me that it could have something to do with our cavemen ancestors needing to be able to identify one another from great distances when hunting (which the women didn't do) but it was much more likely to be 'because of the primary function of hair: that it grows on those parts of the body that are most vulnerable and thus need protection. The differing roles of men and women would help to explain why they have growth in different areas of their bodies.'

Is it possible to knock yourself out using just your own fist?

As anyone who has watched two evenly matched boxers slugging it out over 15 rounds knows, it's hard enough to knock someone else out – let alone to do it to yourself. But does that mean that it is impossible?

I phoned my friend William Mulcahy, who is the cleverest man I know.

'It's possible – just – but almost inevitably it couldn't happen. Let me explain. Human beings are complex, yet also simple. Our species would soon become extinct if we didn't have basic reflexes that prevented us hurting ourselves.

'Punching yourself requires you to suspend a reflex – the reflex that makes you recoil from something painful. The instinct to stay alive can be beaten by the intellect, but you cannot beat reflexes. For example, try falling forward without bringing your hands out to break your fall: it's impossible. In the same way, you would find it impossible to knock yourself out using your own fist – if you were stupid enough to try in the first place. Even if you could override your survival instinct, you wouldn't be able to override your reflex to avoid pain. Instinct and reflex combined would thwart you.'

What do the letters H and B on pencils stand for?

According to a graphic artist friend of mine, 'The H stands for "hardness" and the B for "blackness".'

So why do pencils have both H and B?

'Because a standard pencil has a balance of hardness and blackness. Another pencil might be 4B, meaning very dark and thick. Or you might have a 3H, which would be faint, but sharp and fine.'

I get it – I think.

'Look, I'll make it easier for you. Think of the B not as black but as "soft". Then you're looking at the difference between hard and soft. The more H, the harder and finer the pencil. The more B, the softer and thicker it is.'

Is it true that elephants have good memories?

According to a keeper of elephants at London Zoo, yes, because relative to other animals they have big brains – although not as big as ours.

'They have a good memory,' says the keeper. 'If you teach them to do something, they can still do it a few years later. There are also stories of elephants repaying acts of cruelty and kindness up to thirty years later. For example, in India, if a *mahout* (elephant driver) ill-treated an elephant, the elephant would remember him years later and attack him if given the chance.' The line 'elephants never forget' comes from a book by the writer Saki. In his 1910 book, *Reginald on Besetting Sins*, he wrote: 'Women and elephants never forget an injury.'

Why is poo brown?

What gives poo – or, to use its correct name, 'faeces' – its distinct brown colour is a mixture of dead red blood cells (or haemoglobin) and the bile that comes out of the liver and gall bladder.

Babies don't have many dead red blood cells and that's why their poo is green – especially in the first few evacuations.

Foods with lots of fibre – such as sweetcorn and seeds – sometimes pass through our bodies without getting digested so you shouldn't worry if you see them in your poo.

Is it dangerous to wake up a sleepwalker?

Sleepwalking is perfectly normal in children,' says Dr Roland Powell, 'but it should stop by early adulthood. An adult who still walks in their sleep is probably suffering from stress and should see a psychiatrist or a sleep specialist.'

Thanks for that, Doc, but what I want to know is this: is it dangerous to wake up a sleepwalker?

'It would depend on how vigorously you did it. But no, it's not dangerous. Do it gently, if you must. They will be confused, maybe even a little distressed. But it's much better to simply guide them back to bed in their sleep.'

How come birds don't get electrocuted when they perch on electricity wires?

Luckily for me, physicist Dr Adrian Newman was in a good mood when I called him to ask him this question.

'Oh, that's easy,' he starts and rattles off an explanation that goes straight over my head.

Listen, Adrian, can you explain that more simply?

'OK,' he said *very* slowly, 'here's how it works. When a bird stands on a wire, it gets an electric charge but it doesn't get electrocuted because no current flows through it. The bird doesn't complete a circuit. Do you understand?'

No.

'All right, look at it this way. Electricity is lazy. It wants to travel as quickly and as easily as possible from one side of the generator to the other. A bird, however, isn't a good conductor and it doesn't offer the current a quick way home. Why would electricity want to bother going up one skinny leg, through the bird's body and out through the other skinny leg when it can just carry along on its path, ignoring the bird's tiny claw? Now, a human hand would be different: it would make a fine conductor and so the human would get electrocuted. Do you understand now?'

Er, no.

'Well, don't worry, your readers will.'

Why is a yawn so infectious?

I asked social anthropologist Dr Lorraine Mackintosh.

'As everyone knows,' she told me, 'human beings tend to copy each other's body language. So if one person does something, their companion will often do it too, perhaps without knowing. This dates back to our Stone Age days, when we did everything in groups. The yawn would be a signal that it was time to start winding down and go to sleep. Fast-forward thousands of years and, of course, we don't all need to go to sleep at the same time. However, the instinct remains, so that if someone yawns, other people will find themselves yawning too.'

Why would anyone want to 'pop' a weasel?

You know the old nursery rhyme 'Pop Goes the Weasel'?

Half a pound of tuppenny rice,
Half a pound of treacle.
That's the way the money goes,
Pop! goes the weasel.

Well, it derives from the mid 19th century, when 'to pop' meant to take something to the pawnbroker's to raise money. Indeed, the second verse of the song name-checks the City Road in London, which had a well-known pawnbroker's. As for the weasel, that's rhyming slang for 'coat' – as in 'weasel and stoat' = coat.

What is the oldest trick in the book?

People I spoke to reckoned that it was 'any trick you've fallen for that your best friend hasn't. He can be guaranteed to say, "That's the oldest trick in the book," just to rub it in.'

Someone else said it was Satan's deception of Adam and Eve. The serpent told Eve in the Garden of Eden, 'If you will eat of that tree over there, you will be like God. You will be as wise as He is.' So Eve ate the fruit, gave some to Adam and they were kicked out of Eden. Consequently, this is the oldest trick in the book – or, rather, the Book – i.e. the Bible.

Me? I still reckon that putting shaving cream in a friend's hand and then tickling his nose takes some beating . . .

Swans don't sing, so why do we talk about a performer giving their 'swan song'?

It is true that swans don't sing, but there is a legend that they get to sing a single song just before they die. From this incorrect (but charming) myth, we get the idea of a 'swan song' – an actor's or singer's final performance.

Why in Britain and Commonwealth countries do we drive on the left when in other countries they drive on the right?

Wrong question! It should be: Why do other countries drive on the right when we drive on the left?

Let me explain. Travelling on the left is the way it has always been – long before cars were invented. And why? Because as you were walking or riding your horse, you needed to know that you could draw your sword – with your right hand – if the person passing by on the other side of the road turned out to be hostile.

The big change came just after the French Revolution in 1789. The leaders of the new France wanted to change everything – even the calendar, though that change didn't last.

One of the changes they made was to drive on the right. The United States of America – which won its War of Independence against the British at much the same time – was influenced by France and opted for a similar system. Much of the world subsequently followed the example set by the Americans and the French.

Why, when someone is dismissed from their job, are they 'given the sack'?

I phoned linguist Dr Karen Landy, who told me, 'In medieval times workers would carry all their tools around with them in a sack. They would leave the empty sack at the premises where they were working. If the employer decided to dismiss them, he would then hand them their sack so that they could pack up their tools and go. Thus, they were "given the sack".'

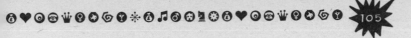

Why is someone described as being 'under the weather' – especially when the weather's fine?

This is a nautical term. In days gone by, when someone felt seasick, they were advised to go below and find a spot in the middle of the ship where the motion would be much less noticeable. In that way they were 'under the weather'.

Why are policemen called coppers?

I wanted to believe that the word 'cop' was an abbreviation of 'constable on patrol'. But no. It turns out that it comes from the verb 'to cop', meaning to arrest or to seize.

How deep is the sea?

The deepest part of the ocean is believed to be the Mariana Trench, south-east of Japan. This trench reaches a depth of 11,035 metres. Compare this to the height of Mount Everest at 8,848 metres.

Below a few thousand metres, there's no light or algae and therefore no energy. There's also very little oxygen. The few fish that can live that deep are usually blind and have huge mouths so that they can eat any food – possibly bones – that might come their way.

Why do we say 'many happy returns' to someone on their birthday?

It's short for 'many happy returns of the day' – that is to say, 'may this day return many times' or 'may you have many more birthdays'.

What makes feet smell like cheese?

I needed to speak to an expert and so I visited Mrs Winwood, my local chiropodist (foot doctor).

'As I understand it,' she said, 'the same bacteria that are found in smelly feet – not yours, of course – are also used in the making of cheese. Not *precisely* the same bacteria, but similar ones, and they produce a similar smell. But what we enjoy in food, we don't necessarily appreciate in feet.'

So what can you do about smelly feet?

'Apart from changing socks regularly – even more than once a day if you sweat a lot – you could also try sprinkling boracic acid powder on your feet and footwear. You can get this from the chemist's. My other advice is to change your shoes regularly. If you wear the same pair day after day, they don't get a chance to air.'

What is the origin of the expression 'OK'?

There are several different possibilities.

1. Obadiah Kelly – a US railroad freight agent, who marked his initials on important papers to show that everything was in order.

2. *Okeh* – the Choctaw word for 'yes'.

3. 'Orl Korect' or 'Oll Korrect' – 19th-century US president Andrew Jackson's folksy way of expressing himself, which led to him being known as O.K. Jackson.

4. Old Kinderhook – President Jackson's successor, Martin Van Buren, joined in the 'OK' fun and used the initials to refer to his hometown of Kinderhook.

5. *Olla Kalla* – the Greek expression for 'all is good'.

6. *O Ke* – in Mandingo (a West African language) means 'all right'.

7. *Wav Kay* – in Wolof (another West African language) means 'yes indeed'.

8. *Omnia Correctes* – in Latin means 'all is correct'.

9. *Aux Cayes* (pronounced 'OK') – a place in Haiti.

10. *Och Aye* – in Scottish means 'oh yes'.

11. *Oc* – is derived from the Latin affirmative hoc.

It's hard to know which explanation is the true one – although I lean towards a combination of 3 and 4. What we *can* say for certain is that President Van Buren popularized the expression so that by the 1840s it was being widely used.

OK OK OK OK

OK OK OK OK OK OK

Why do we tell someone who is getting angry to keep their shirt on?

This goes back to the days when gentlemen who had decided to have a fight would first take off their shirts. Consequently, telling someone to 'keep your shirt on' became a way of trying to stop a fight. Nowadays, no man considering having a fight would strip to the waist, but his friends might still advise him to keep his shirt on.

It's an example of a saying outliving its origins.

Will a sleeping person wet the bed if you dip his or her hand in warm water?

This is one prank that can work a treat! I asked Dr Roland Powell how it works.

'Mostly, it's the power of suggestion – to which we are most vulnerable when we're asleep. Just the thought – or sound – of water will encourage us to pee during the day, so when your hand is plunged into water at night, it can have an extraordinary effect. It is the combination of the water (which encourages peeing) and the shock (which is conducive to making you let go – in this case of your bladder). And, as you know, if you're having a tough time peeing, just letting the water run in a nearby sink works too.'

Why is an Academy Award in the United States known as an Oscar?

No one knows for sure. There are three possible explanations:

1. A newspaper columnist, Sidney Skolsky, thought the official name – the Academy Award of Merit – was too pretentious and called it an Oscar (after an old joke).

2. The actress Bette Davis thought that the statue's bottom reminded her of her husband Harmon Oscar Nelson's.

3. This is the most likely possibility: the academy's librarian, Margaret Herrick, saw the statue and exclaimed, 'It looks just like my uncle Oscar!'

How many is 'umpteen'?

The word 'umpteen' is a slang term for an unspecified but large number. It is generally used for fun, as though it is not worth the effort to pin down the true figure. Usually it refers to the number of times something has happened, rather than a number of objects.

'Umpteen' possibly comes from 'umpty', a military slang version of the Morse Code dash used to show an indefinite number. Although 'teen' is added to the end, 'umpteen' is almost always used for a number much bigger than 13 to 19.

Why do trousers come in pairs?

Because legs do!

Are guinea pigs ever used as guinea pigs?

Disappointingly, for those of us who like things to do what they say on the tin, it seems that guinea pigs are very rarely used as, er, guinea pigs. Nowadays, rats and mice are preferred, because they're smaller, cheaper to feed and reproduce more quickly. They're also easier to manipulate genetically. And, of course, they don't have the same cuddly image as guinea pigs do.

However, guinea pigs have an immune system similar to ours and, like us, don't synthesize their own vitamin C. They also have incredibly sensitive skin that shows up potential allergens immediately.

The interesting thing about guinea pigs is that they're neither from Guinea, which of course is in Africa, and nor are they pigs. They are cavies (cuddly rodents). The creatures originated in South America more than 3,000 years ago. When the Spanish conquered the

Incas in the 16th century, they brought guinea pigs over to Europe via the port of Guinea (hence their name). In Peru people still eat guinea pigs and keep them in their gardens rather like we keep chickens.

What bits of a pig and/or cow go into sausages?

I once met a guy who had worked in a factory where they made sausages. When I asked him what went into them, he simply shook his head and said, 'Put it this way, I've never eaten one since.' This only put me off for a while. The next time I smelled frying sausages, I was ready to eat them again.

So I phoned the major sausage manufacturers and they all suggested I read the list of ingredients on the packet. When I pushed the point, one of them said:

'Look, of course we use the bits of meat that can't be sold for other purposes – as steak or pork chops – but how good, how lean, the meat is depends on the price you pay for the sausages. But you'll never find anything really nasty, like bits of rat or hair, because what would be in it for us? Why would we do that?'

What about all the gribbly bits of animals?

'I don't deny that we use gristle and fat, but since September 2002 retailers have been obliged to have clear labels showing

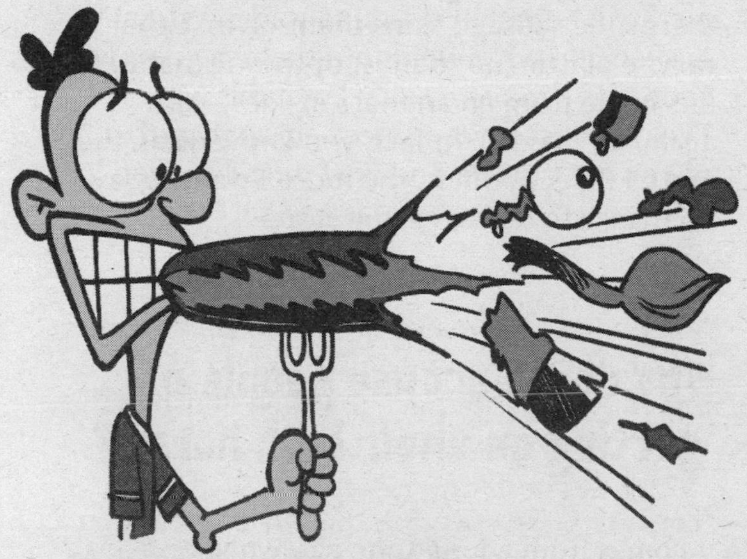

customers the meat content in sausages and burgers. And only flesh with permitted levels of gristle, cartilage and fat will count as meat. Animal fat, gristle and skin in excess of those levels, and offal, now have to be shown as separate to the meat.'

I suppose I'm reassured, although even the supposedly reasonable added ingredients – like rusk, protein concentrate, polyphosphate, monosodium glutamate, cochineal and sodium metabisulphite – give me pause for thought. More to the point, there's the sausage skins themselves. Either they're plastic (no thanks) or they're 'natural' (i.e. made from an animal's insides – and again, no thanks). In fact, you know what, the more I think about it, the more I want to say no thanks to sausages, full stop.

Why do we accuse people of 'getting on their high horse'?

It comes from a long time ago when a person's rank – i.e. their position in society – was determined by the height of their horse (and a high horse indicated a superior person).

What would happen to the passengers if someone opened the emergency exit of an aeroplane while it was in the air?

In theory – as all James Bond film fans will remember – the passengers would all be sucked out, especially if they weren't wearing seat belts. So what protection is there against this? I asked my friend Terry, who is a pilot. Did he ever worry about a drunken passenger opening the emergency exit, for example?

'Never. What you have to know is that an aeroplane door opens in, not out. Now, on the ground – where the door is meant to be opened – this makes no difference because the air pressure is the same inside and out. But when you are in the air, it does make a difference. The higher you go, the thinner the air. This means that the cabin has to be pressurized, or else everyone would die from lack of oxygen. The difference between the pressure outside and the pressure inside makes it impossible to open the emergency exit – or, indeed, the regular doors, because although they open out, they first have to be pulled in a bit, which is impossible at altitude. So there's nothing to worry about.'

Why is it easier to park a car backwards than forwards?

I am a terrible driver so I asked my mate Rob to explain.

He said, 'When you turn a car's steering wheel it moves the *front* wheels. Therefore, if you get the back end of the car into the parking space first, the trickier part can be

done with the end over which you have greater control: the front. For the same reason, it is much easier to get out of a parking space forwards.'

Is that it?

'Yes.'

So why do I find parking so difficult?

'Because you're an idiot.'

Why do we say 'bless you' when someone sneezes?

During the Great Plague of London (1664–1665), people were always looking for a sign of plague (in themselves and in others) and they decided that sneezing was an early indication. So, if someone sneezed, they

would immediately say, 'God bless you' or, 'Bless you'. The link between sneezing and the plague is also found in the nursery rhyme 'Ring a Ring o' Roses', which contains the line: 'atishoo atishoo, we all fall down' – or: 'sneeze, sneeze, we all drop dead'.

Interestingly, every time we sneeze, our hearts stop for a fraction of a second!

What is the best way to cure hiccups?

No one knows precisely how hiccups are caused – eating, drinking, talking, laughing, swallowing air, anxiety are all possibilities – but they are annoying, even if they do provide merriment for everyone else.

Anyway, here is a list of cures that someone somewhere swears by:

• Eating a tablespoon of peanut butter.

• Pinching your nose while you drink water.

• Pinching the back of your shoulder until it hurts (this works because the nerves that control your diaphragm come from the same place).

• Exhaling as hard as you can and then holding your breath.

- Coughing or sneezing.
- Swallowing a teaspoon of sugar.
- Holding the tongue with your thumb and index finger and gently pulling it forwards.

- Getting someone to drop an ice cube down your back.
- Laughing.
- Deliberately *trying* to hiccup as much as possible (you might even persuade a friend to *pay* you for each hiccup).

- Breathing into a paper bag.
- Chewing gum.
- Immersing your face in iced water.
- Gargling.
- Drinking a glass of water while someone presses your ears closed.

My own favourite is drinking water from the far side of a glass (so that you're drinking upside down). Well, it works for me.

A Bactrian camel has two humps; a dromedary has just one. If a Bactrian and a dromedary were to breed, would their offspring have one hump or two?

Long question, short answer: one. We know this because Bactrians and dromedaries are regularly cross-bred. Cross-bred camels are excellent beasts that combine all the best attributes of the two breeds. The only trouble is that these cross-breeds are sterile, and so every time more are wanted, they have to get one of each breed and – this is only a guess – put on some smoochy, romantic music.

HUMP-
FREY

My local supermarket is open 24 hours a day, 365 days a year – so why are there locks on the doors?

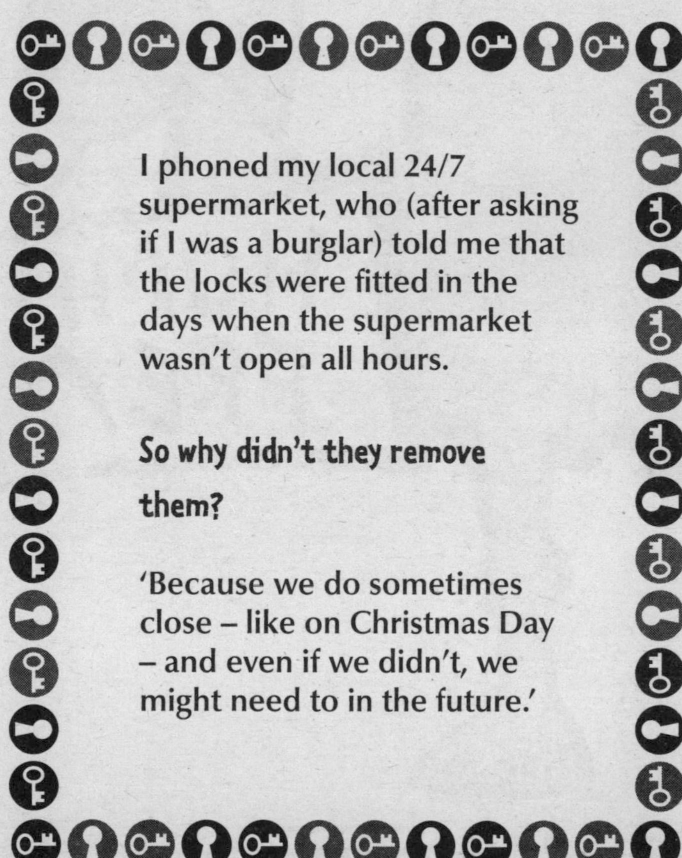

I phoned my local 24/7 supermarket, who (after asking if I was a burglar) told me that the locks were fitted in the days when the supermarket wasn't open all hours.

So why didn't they remove them?

'Because we do sometimes close – like on Christmas Day – and even if we didn't, we might need to in the future.'

How do you explain crop circles?

I don't. They're all spoofs.

Really?

Yes, no question.

Which came first – the chicken or the egg?

According to Genesis, the chicken came first, but scientists over at *National Geographic* magazine have been considering this thorny

old question and have come down firmly on the side of the egg. Apparently, reptiles were laying eggs thousands of years before chickens ever appeared. What happened was that one day (a long time ago) an egg that was not quite a chicken's egg was laid by a bird that was not quite a chicken. Evolution took over from there.

Why do we shake hands as a greeting?

I am not a great hand-shaker. Not since I read somewhere that colds and other viruses are passed on by this kind of physical contact. Besides, the reason we shake hands has nothing to do with warmth or kindness and everything to do with mistrust. So we shake hands to check for concealed weapons. This goes back to the Middle Ages, when two

men would extend their right hands – their weapon hands – to show that they weren't carrying daggers.

Shaking hands has another function: to seal a deal – 'Let's shake hands on it.' Here, people are not checking for weapons but are entering into a symbolic union. In ancient times shaking hands was a sort of basic magic that signified two people giving in to one another. Shaking and clasping hands also played a big part in ancient wedding ceremonies.

Is it wrong to prompt a stutterer?

I have a neighbour named Stephen who sometimes stutters. He doesn't stutter all the time but when he does – usually when he's being rushed or when he's nervous – he's very hard to understand. Like most stutterers, he has trouble with his Ss, which makes it unfortunate that his parents named him

Stephen. Instinctively, I've never finished one of his sentences, but was I wrong?

'No, you're absolutely right,' said Stephen when I plucked up the courage to ask him. 'Stuttering – or stammering, as we also call it – is embarrassing for both the stutterer and the person he's talking to, but, unless you've got a stutterer's permission, you shouldn't finish his sentences for him. Also you shouldn't tell a stutterer to "slow down", "take a deep breath" or, worst of all, "relax". We know we're stuttering – we don't need you to remind us.'

But you're not stuttering now.

'That's because we're talking face to face and there's no pressure on me. If this were a telephone conversation, I'd be all tangled up. Mind you, it can be funny. A waiter in a restaurant asked me what I wanted with my fish and I said, "Sal – sal – sal—" and for once I was praying for him to finish my sentence, but he didn't. So I ended up asking for chips – which, secretly, was what I wanted anyway, not salad!'

Who was Dr Pepper in the drink of the same name?

Dr Pepper was created in 1885, making it the oldest manufactured soft drink in the States. It was originally made in Morrison's Old Corner Drug Store in Waco, Texas. Wade Morrison, the owner of the store, named it after a Dr Charles Pepper, the Virginia doctor who had given him his first job.

Why 'as cool as a cucumber'?

Yes, why not as cool as a tomato or as cool as a beetroot?

There's a good reason why the cucumber is used as the epitome of cool. However hot or cold the weather is, the middle of a cucumber – its core – is usually some 11°C (20°F) colder than the outside temperature.

If woollen clothes can shrink in the wash, how come sheep don't shrink in sheep dip?

According to an expert from the British Wool Marketing Board, 'There is a molecular difference between "dead" wool (as used in clothes) and "live" wool (which is attached to a living thing). Apart from that, they do now put a chemical in wool which helps stop shrinkage. You must also remember that sheep are dipped in cold water whereas clothes are washed in warm water. For the same reason, sheep don't shrink in the rain.'

So although we are cleverer than sheep, when wool is being worn by them it doesn't shrink, but when it's worn by us, especially in a rainstorm, it can and does shrink.

Why are dusters yellow?

I had to ring around quite a bit to get an answer to this one. This is what one helpful man told me:

'There are many reasons why the dusters we use are yellow. Yellow is a cheerful colour. Dirt shows up more easily against yellow than against most other colours. And using this colour helps us to distinguish dusters from other things when they are in the wash.

'However, it is also a matter of tradition. In the 17th century Europe suffered many outbreaks of plague. Sailors were particularly likely to catch it and pass it on because they travelled so much. Ships were therefore required to fly a yellow flag when coming into ports. This flag, known as the "Yellow Duster", signalled that the ship was free from plague. So the colour yellow became synonymous with cleanliness.'

What is sleepy dust and why do we get it?

When we are awake, we blink every few seconds, releasing a tiny tear that spreads into a film of water to protect the eyeball – keeping it clean and moist. Tiny specks of dust and other particles of rubbish get washed away.

When we are asleep, we are not blinking and producing tears to wash away stuff and so it accumulates in the corners of our eyes, where it becomes (what we call) sleepy dust.

Why is someone who is being ignored 'sent to Coventry'?

Like so many expressions, this one has all sorts of possible explanations.

One possibility is that the name Coventry derives from 'Cofa's tree'. Cofa was a leader in the 11th or 12th century and the tree was where he hanged his victims. A neat way of sending someone to Coventry, as I'm sure you'd agree.

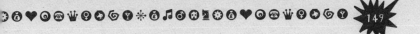

Another possibility is that Coventry was the first major town where fugitives from the Bow Street Runners (a pre-19th-century police force) could rest because it was just outside the area they policed.

However, the best explanation is that during the 17th-century English Civil War, Royalist prisoners were sent to jail in Coventry. The locals didn't like them and would ignore them. Hence being 'sent to Coventry' meant to be ignored.

How is it that we can get a headache from eating ice cream too quickly?

An ice-cream headache is an unpleasant experience. It only lasts for about 25 seconds but that doesn't matter because when it hits, it's really terrible. Interestingly, it is also the number one cause of headaches – and affects a third of the population – but only occurs in warm weather.

According to Mr Jonathan Leigh, a consultant neurologist (a doctor dealing with the nervous system), 'When something cold touches the roof of your mouth, it causes the blood vessels in your head to dilate. There's a nerve centre just above the roof of your mouth. When this gets cold, it overreacts and tries to heat the brain, thus causing a stabbing or aching pain known as "brain freeze". The best way to avoid this is to keep your ice cream or ice lolly away from the roof of your mouth.'

Is it dangerous?

'No. Unpleasant for the few seconds you experience it but not at all dangerous, unless it triggers a migraine, which it might in some people. Those people should think twice before sucking anything very cold.'

Who sent the first email? When? What did it say?

Ray Tomlinson sent the first email, in 1971, to another computer in the same room in Cambridge, Massachusetts. The message was something like QWERTYUIOP – the keys across the top line of the keyboard.

The first message of any substance was one announcing that network mail was available. It gave instructions about using the @ sign to separate the user's name from the host computer name. In other words, the first use of network email was to announce its own existence.

'Why email?' said Ray. 'That would be a more interesting question. And the answer is simply that it seemed like a neat idea. It was a solution looking for a problem.'

Ray chose the @ sign because 'the sign didn't appear in names, so there would be no confusion about where the user name ended and the host name began'.

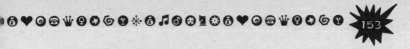

How did marmalade get its name?

I had always believed the old wives' tale that marmalade got its name because the Scottish woman who invented it asked her son if he would like some 'more my lad' – and this expression became 'marmalade'. Well, it's as good an answer as any for something that should simply be called orange jam.

Anyway, it turns out that the nation's favourite breakfast spread owes its name to the fact that it comes from Portugal, where quince jam was known as *marmelada*. At about the same time that oranges became popular in Britain, the word *marmelada* was translated into English to apply to all jams, but it only stuck to orange jam.

If you cut a worm in half, does it become two worms?

Yes and no, according to my old pal Lucy, who used to work at the Natural History Museum.

Hmm, that's not very helpful, old pal.

'Well, it's complicated.'

Not for you, surely?

'No, dummy, for you!'

Tell us what happens.

'Well, you *do* get two moving parts but they are still the same worm. The front of the garden worm can generate a new tail, but the tail can't find a new head, and so the tail dies – after wriggling around for a while. However, the flatworm – found near water – can be cut into two or even three parts and each bit will grow a new head and/or tail.'

Is it true that eating carrots can help you see in the dark?

Yes. Carrots contain carotene, which the body uses to make vitamin A, which is good for your eyesight – especially for seeing in the dark.

But let me make it clear: nothing can help you see in pitch-black. Also the chances are you have got enough vitamin A in your body, so extra carrots would make no difference to your night vision. But around the world, especially in countries where the diet is poor, lack of vitamin A is a leading cause of blindness.

Too much vitamin A is as bad for you as too little. It is possible to overdose, but it is very hard to do so.

Why is French bread so long?

According to historian Dr Michael Morgan, during the Napoleonic Wars 'French soldiers had to be able to carry their bread as they travelled on foot, but they didn't have very much space in their knapsacks. So some bright spark – and legend says it was Napoleon himself – suggested that bakers make very long sticks of bread so that the men could shove it down their trousers and carry it like that.'

Which is the most filmed story of all time?

I would have guessed *Cinderella* but in fact the answer is *Dracula* (written by Bram Stoker) – followed by *Dr Jekyll and Mr Hyde* (Robert Louis Stevenson) and then *Oliver Twist* (Charles Dickens).

Interestingly, although most of the films based on these stories were made in the US (in Hollywood), all three were by writers from Britain and Ireland.

Why do men's jackets have buttons on the cuffs?

There's a simple but silly answer to this: they were originally put on male servants' cuffs by their employers to stop them wiping their noses on the sleeves of their uniforms. Tailors thought it looked smart and so the buttons were put on men's suits. That's it.

Why do we say 'as sick as a parrot'?

I found two possible explanations for this, and you can take your pick.

It's either a version of the expression 'as sick as a *pierrot*' – as in a French clown – or (and this is the one I prefer) it's a contraction of the northern expression 'as sick as a parrot with a broken beak'.

Why are British stamps the only stamps in the world that don't carry the name of their country of origin?

Because the British invented the modern postage stamp (in 1840), they have this special concession – but only on the understanding that the monarch's head appears on each stamp.

How many people need to be in the same room to make it probable that two of them will share the same birthday?

This is, in fact, a trick question – although the maths required to work it out is completely on the level. Your immediate reaction might be to say 365 people, one for every day of a non-leap year. Then, after seeing the word 'probable', you think, OK, let's divide that by two and then add one – just to make it slightly more probable: 183.

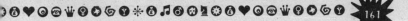

Incredibly, the answer turns out to be not 365 or 183, but 23. That's right, you only need 23 people gathered together to make it *probable* that two of them will share the same birthday.

So I asked my friend William Mulcahy, an actuary who got a first in maths at university, to give me the lowdown.

'First, consider the case that 23 people do *not* have a birthday in common. There are 365 x 365 x 365 x 365 . . . (365 multiplied by itself 23 times) ways in which 23 birthdays can be chosen; some of these may be the same. However, there are only 365 x 364 x 363 x 362 x 361 x 360 x 359 x 358 x 357 x 356 x 355 x 354 x 353 x 352 x 351 x 350 x 349 x 348 x 347 x 346 x 345 x 344 x 343 ways in which 23 birthdays can be chosen without any being the same. The reason for this is that there are 365 ways of choosing the first birthday; after this has been chosen, there are 364 ways of choosing the second birthday, and so on. Dividing the number of ways in which 23 birthdays can be chosen without being the same by the number of ways in which 23 birthdays can be chosen with some being the same gives us the mathematical probability of 23 people *not* having a birthday in common as 0.493. This means that the probability of at least two of the 23 people *having* a birthday in common is greater: 0.507.

'It's only when you get to 23 that the probability of a shared birthday becomes greater than the probability of no birthday being shared. So if there are 23 or more people in the same room, it is more likely that at least two of them have the same birthday than it is that they do not have a birthday in common.'

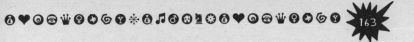

Oh, of course.

'But remember that although there only have to be 23 people present to make it probable that any two share the same birthday, if you specify the date of the birthday they share – say 11 February – then there have to be 253 people present to make it probable. I can give you the maths if you like.'

Er, no thank you.

Is it dangerous to swallow chewing gum?

As we all know, chewing gum is the most disgusting substance known to man. However, Dr Roland Powell says that everything you have ever heard about the dangers of chewing gum, and of swallowing it, is untrue.

All of it?

'All of it.'

So it doesn't take seven years to digest, or wind itself round the alimentary canal, or end up in your appendix?

'Absolute rubbish. Of course, chewing gum is indigestible, but then so is quite a lot of the stuff we eat – grape pips and watermelon seeds, for example. All that happens is that the chewing gum passes through the digestive system as roughage. I should say, however, that chewing gum during bouts of vigorous exercise is not a good idea. If you swallowed the gum the wrong way, it could stop you breathing and kill you.'

But apart from that?

'Well, it's not good for young children to swallow too much of it because it can clog up the digestive tract. One infant was rewarded with chewing gum during toilet-training sessions and it caused him to be constipated for two days.'

If Jesus Christ hadn't been born, what would the date be in 2007?

First off, it shouldn't be 2007 as Jesus wasn't born when you think he was: it was some time between 4 BC and AD 13. He wasn't born on Christmas Day for that matter, either.

But, assuming that Jesus hadn't been born– and assuming that we had adopted the Roman calendar – then the year would now be 2760. The alternative is that we would have adopted a calendar based on the Old Testament, which, working from Bishop Usher's date (4004 BC), would make it 6011.

Do dolphins sleep?

Yes, according to a marine biologist I know, but it is not sleep as we know it.' Dolphins and other sea mammals have brains that allow them to swim with or against the current 24 hours a day, without being swept away or drowning. How it works is that their brains have two hemispheres, or halves. Each hemisphere takes it in turn to "sleep", while the other stays alert to keep the creature safe.'

Why are German measles 'German'?

There is a long and terrible tradition of countries describing unpleasant things and practices in terms of foreigners. Consequently, my immediate instinct was that we called Rubella (the medical name for the disease) 'German Measles' as a way of insulting and blaming the Germans.

In fact, the name has nothing to do with the country and everything to do with the corruption of words. The word 'German' is a corruption of *germane* – meaning alike or akin to – measles, the viral illness to which it is related. German measles is not usually a problem for men but it can have awful effects on an unborn child if a woman catches it during the early months of pregnancy – which is why all of us, men and women, have compulsory vaccinations against it.

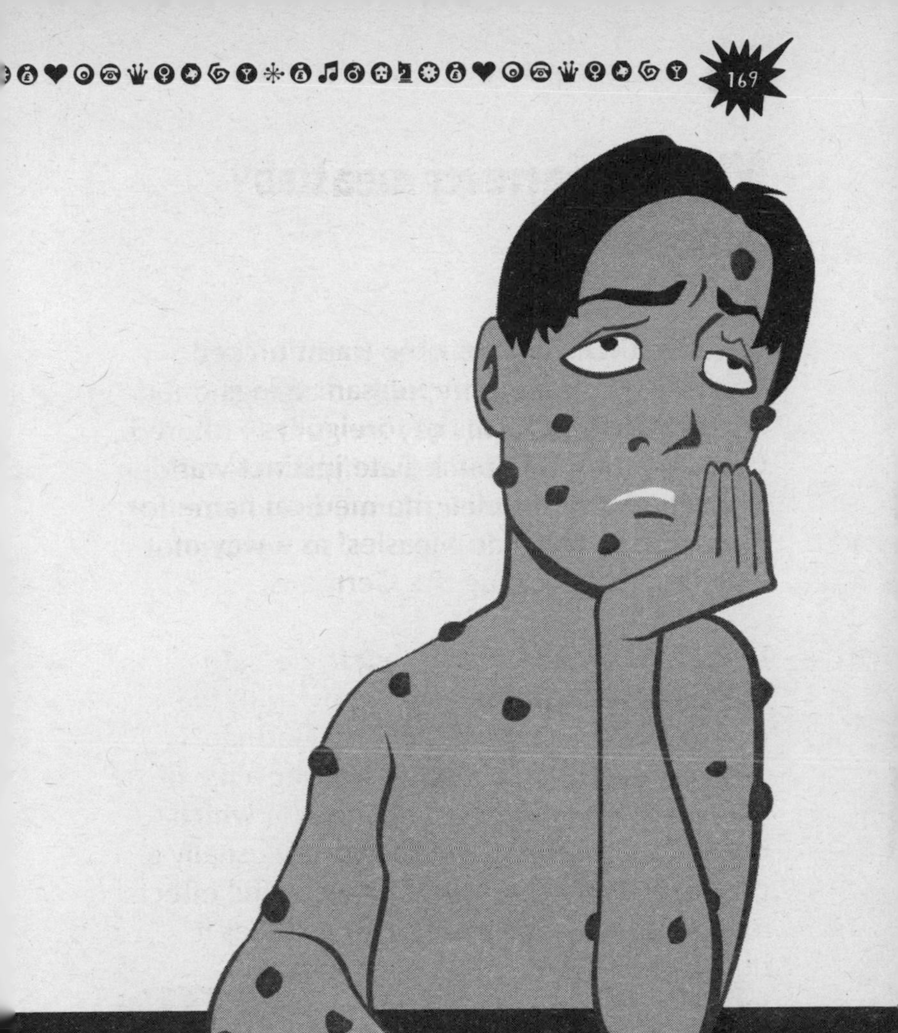

Why do we never see baby pigeons?

Because their parents keep them tucked away. Little pigeons are looked after and fed by their parents until they are fully feathered, and only then do they leave their well-hidden nest. By this time, their plumage and size is the same as an adult pigeon's, so we cannot tell the difference.

Why do golf courses have 18 holes?

In fact, it's only when you stop to think about it that you realize that 18 is a random number – unless you live on the Planet Plog, where they operate a counting system based on the figure nine. However, there is a good reason.

The Old Course at St Andrews was where it all started, and this was originally just 12 holes. Golfers used to finish their round and then play it in reverse – cutting out two of the holes – thus playing a 22-hole round. Then, in 1764, the chaps from St Andrews decided that the first four holes were too short and so these were turned into two holes. Take off two holes going out and two going in and you have 18 holes. And where St Andrews led, all other golf courses – including, eventually, everywhere else in the world – followed.

Why are Liverpudlians known as Scousers?

According to my good friend Keiran, a native of Liverpool, the word 'scouse' derives from the traditional dish eaten on Merseyside. This stew – made from mutton or fish and potatoes, carrots and onions – was introduced to the area by sailors from either Germany (where it was known as *Labskaus*) or Norway (where there was a similar dish called *Lab Skaas*). Originally known as lobscouse, this was eventually shortened to scouse, and the people who ate it were therefore known as Scousers.

What is the origin of the V-sign?

There are of course two V-signs. There's Churchill's one, denoting victory, in which the palm of the hand is shown, and then there's – well, there's the other one. However, the 'naughty' V-sign has origins just as noble as the nice one. I learned this from the historian Dr Michael Morgan. 'The V-sign has its origins in the Battle of Agincourt. The French threatened to cut off the bow fingers of the English archers if they won the battle. So when instead England won, the victors flicked V-signs at the losers, to show they still had all their fingers.'

We know that cats can fall or jump from great heights and survive, but how high? Could a cat survive a fall from, say, the 19th floor of a building?

I am *not* a cat lover. Sorry, but that's how it is. The world is split on dogs and cats, and I'm with the dogs.

Anyway, that doesn't answer the question. I asked both a vet and a physicist and between them they gave me the answer. Cats *can* survive great falls, but they have a better chance of survival the higher up they are – up to a certain point. If a cat falls off the sixth floor of a building, it has *less* chance of surviving than a cat that falls off, say, the 19th. It takes about eight floors for the cat to understand what's happening so that it can relax and prepare itself for the fall. If the cat is not prepared, it will hit the ground at maximum speed and be splattered over the pavement.

Could som*on* writ* an *ntir* nov*l without onc* using th* l*tt*r 'e'?

Yes. A man called Ernest Vincent Wright wrote a book in 1939, called *Gadsby*, in which he never used the letter 'e'. (Apart from in his name on the cover, I imagine . . .) Amazing! And it was a good book by all accounts.

The author didn't cheat. Just think how difficult it would be to write a story never using pronouns such as 'he', 'she', 'they' and 'we', never using any word ending in -ed – not to mention the word 'the'. Have a go yourself and you will see what an extraordinary achievement it was. Sadly, Wright, who took 165 days to write it – simply to prove that it could be done – died on the day the book was published.

Why do we clink glasses when we say 'cheers'?

This dates back to the days when people sometimes attempted to poison their enemies. To prove that a drink was safe, a host would pour some of his guest's wine into his own glass and drink it first. Later, this evolved into crashing tankards together so that a little of both drinks spilt into each other. Eventually, guests and hosts would demonstrate their friendship for each other by touching – or clinking – glasses. By clinking, they showed that they were aware of the possibility of poisoning, but by doing it so lightly, they were showing their trust.

Why are sports matches between local teams always called derbies?

The Earl of Derby, who gave his name to the annual horse race the Derby, which takes place at Epsom in Surrey, also liked to challenge local landowners to race their horses against his. These races became 'Derby's', or derbies.

Why do burglars wear striped polo-neck jerseys and carry bags marked 'Swag'?

This goes back to the end of the 18th century, when sailors in the Royal Navy, who wore striped jerseys, were notorious for being thieves. It wasn't their fault. They were badly paid when working, and then discharged from service with absolutely nothing. The pantomime eye mask was probably invented by the cartoonists of the time.

The word 'swag' is possibly a combination of 'to sway' and 'to sag' – in the way a bag loaded with stolen things might do.

Why is New York known as the Big Apple?

There are three possibilities:

1. In 1909 Edward S. Martin wrote in his book, *The Wayfarer in New York*: 'New York [was] merely one of the fruits of that great tree whose roots go down in the Mississippi Valley, and whose branches spread from one ocean to the other . . . [But] the big apple [New York] gets a disproportionate share of the national sap.'

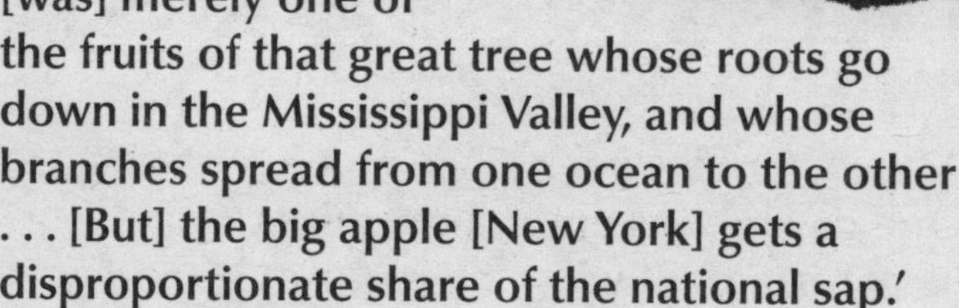

2. Another possibility is that it comes from a mistranslation. In Spanish, the word *manzana* can mean 'block' (a small section of a town or city) or 'apple'. So when immigrants referred to New York as 'the Big Block', people thought they were calling it 'the Big Apple'.

3. The third possibility is that it derives from jazz musicians' slang. In the 1920s they used to refer to gigs as 'apples' and New York was, of course, the big apple. The phrase was also used in other walks of life – for example, stable hands – to mean 'the big time'. A newspaper sports writer John J. FitzGerald heard it and called his racing column 'Around the Big Apple', which would have helped to popularize the expression.

Who first thought of using credit cards?

A New York lawyer named Frank McNamara. One day he was entertaining guests at a local restaurant when he realized he had left his money at home. While he waited for someone to go and fetch some money, he reckoned there had to be an alternative solution. So, in 1950, he started the Diner's Club, with just 200 card-holders.

Do two wrongs make a right?

My feeling is that two wrongs *don't* make a right. If someone does something wrong to you, you might enjoy doing something wrong to them – you might even see it as 'righting a wrong' – but I don't think it can be morally justified.

Feeling out of my depth, I phoned Stuart, my friend with a degree in philosophy, and asked him what he thought.

'I think you are right,' he said. 'In fact, I *know* you are right. Let me prove it to you. Let's take two people – Tom and Dick. They know each other but are not friends. Tom's house is burgled by an unknown person. This is a wrong, yes? So he goes out and burgles Dick's home – another wrong. Do those two wrongs make a right? Of course not.

'That's easy, though, because of the third person – the burglar. So let's make it more complicated. Tom borrows Dick's mobile phone without his permission. Tom tells himself that he needed the use of a phone, and Dick would do the same anyway. Do these two wrongs make a right? Again, no.

'But that's still not getting to the heart of the question, which is this: if someone wrongs you, are you "right" to wrong them back?

To which I respond with a question: where does it end? What do you think the state is for? To dispense justice: to right wrongs. So if someone wrongs you, you should seek the appropriate remedy in the criminal or civil courts. For the state to punish someone isn't an example of a second wrong: it's a proper corrective remedy.'

But hang on a minute, what about wrongs that fall outside the scope of the courts – ordinary daily acts of unkindness?

'OK, Tom and Dick are now friends who always send each other birthday cards. One year Dick forgets to send one. Tom thinks his friend is wrong. So what should he do?

If he then does not send a card to Dick on his birthday, will he have righted that wrong? On the contrary, I suggest that he will merely have made Dick feel he was "right" in the first place not to send a card to Tom. If Tom *really* wanted to get one over Dick, he would be better off sending a card: it would be the right thing *and* it would make Dick feel rotten.

'Look, I'm not stupid. I do know there are times when revenge – appropriate revenge – is necessary and, if it prevents further wrongs, it might even be a good idea, but that, in itself, doesn't make it right.

'This question has concerned philosophers for years and there are some who would point out the old chestnut: "Would you steal someone's gun – which is a wrong – if you knew it would stop them from going out to kill another person that evening?" But I say that "stealing" – or, more properly, *taking* – that gun wouldn't be a wrong but a corrective action, and corrective actions can almost always be justified.'

Why are matinée performances in theatres almost always in the afternoon, when *matin* means 'morning' in French?

Good question. In the days before proper theatrical lighting, matinées were indeed held in the mornings, with later performances put on in the afternoon or early evenings. As time went by, the word 'matinée' came to be used for the first performance of the day – whenever it was. And once the problems of illumination were solved, the first performance of the day was usually in the afternoon.

Why do we 'bury the hatchet' when we make up?

This goes back to the days when Native American tribes fought with one another.

Eventually, when one side had had enough, they would throw a tomahawk into the ground, and the other side would do likewise. To white settlers who witnessed this, the tomahawk looked like a hatchet, or a small axe, and they coined the expression 'to bury the hatchet' – meaning to end hostilities or to make up.

Why are men's buttons on the left and women's buttons on the right?

In the old days, men dressed themselves, but wealthy women were dressed by their maids. The maids would button them up to the left – that is, using the buttons on the right. So it became standard for the buttons on women's clothes to be on the right.

Where did the Adam's apple get its name from?

You know that lump at the front of a man's neck? Well, that lump – made of thyroid cartilage – is technically called the 'laryngeal prominence' but is much more commonly known as the Adam's apple. Because it's much more prominent in men than in women, it was named after the 'first man' – i.e. Adam – and it was said to be the forbidden apple he consumed, which got stuck in his throat.

Why do we talk about a scapegoat? Why not a scapecow, or a scaperabbit?

This goes back to biblical times, when people would bring two goats to a sacrificial altar. One goat would be slain but the other – said to carry the sins of the congregation – was allowed to escape. Hence the word 'scapegoat'. Shame, really, as I much prefer scapecow but obviously they couldn't get a cow into the church . . .

Why do we clap our hands to show approval?

I turned to social anthropologist Dr Lorraine Mackintosh, who told me: 'It's something our ape ancestors used to do to express pleasure or happiness. Babies and tiny children do it too – although they are also encouraged to do so by imitating their parents.'

But why clapping?

'It fulfils many different functions. When we clap – say at a concert – we are participating by adding our own accompaniment during a song, and then we mark the end of the song by clapping. We are also, at the end of a play or a speech or a song, expressing our approval in a way that can be heard.'

Is that why presenters at concerts tell people to 'make some noise'?

'Yes. How else can human beings – or apes – make noise, apart from with our voices? It's obvious when you stop to think about it.'

Of course.

'This, however, is where it starts to get interesting, because making noise can signify disapproval as well as approval. Nowadays, clapping is usually done positively, but in ancient Greece people clapped to drown out poor performers as well as to applaud good ones. In fact, clapping was so important in Athens that people organized themselves into groups called claques to clap for cash. Drama competitions were won – and lost – on the basis of which actors or playwrights had hired the noisiest claque.'

An early example of an audience voting performers in or out, like today's *Big Brother*?

'Absolutely.'

Who was Larry – and why was he so happy?

We've all heard the expression 'as happy as Larry' but who was this happy chap? Alas, there is no definite answer. Some people say that it refers to the great 20th-century actor, Sir Laurence ('Larry') Olivier, and his relief at leaving a coastal resort where he'd been performing, but this is unlikely. It's probably either short for Lazarus (the man in the Bible who rose from the dead – which would make anyone happy), or for 'larrikin', a term used to describe a roisterer (someone who 'roists' or likes to have a good time).

Where does bellybutton fluff come from and why is it always blue?

The bellybutton – especially one that goes in, rather than protrudes – is a great place for sweat to accumulate. Sweat is sticky, and tiny fibres from the clothes you are wearing, particularly cotton, will adhere to it. These tiny bits of fibre eventually join together to form little balls of lint – or navel fluff. The larger and hairier the bellybutton, the more fluff there will be, which is why this affects grown-ups, mostly men, more than children. Mine yields enough in a month to knit a sweater.

Now for the second part of the question: why is it always blue??

Well, apparently it isn't *always* blue. The colour of navel fluff depends on the colour of cotton clothing a person wears. If someone wears only yellow , their fluff will be yellow. However, most people's fluff is a greyish blue because they wear a number of different colours and greyish blue is what you get when those colours are mixed in the 'paintbox' of the bellybutton.

Why *piggy* banks?

It's because of an old Dutch custom. In the Netherlands, at the beginning of the year, children were given pig-shaped earthenware containers (known as 'feast pigs') to save their pennies in. The following Christmas they got to open them up. From there, we get the piggy bank in which children – or, rather, *good* children – save their money all year round.

Who wrote the song 'Happy Birthday'?

'Happy Birthday' is the most often performed song of all time.

The original song – 'Good Morning to You' – was written in the 1890s by sisters Mildred and Patty Hill but – silly them – they didn't take out a copyright until 1935, by which time it was called 'Happy Birthday'. This copyright doesn't expire until 2011 – but, fortunately, it only applies to commercial performances so there's no problem in singing it on your friends' birthdays.

Why do buses travel in threes?

Well, it is not a cruel trick played by the bus companies just to annoy us. This is what a transport expert I consulted told me:

'If a lot of passengers are at one stop, the bus (Bus 1) that picks them up has to wait quite a long time to get them all on board. This allows the bus behind (Bus 2) to catch up a little. Because Bus 2 arrives faster, there's less time for a queue to build up, so Bus 2 doesn't have to stay there long. Meanwhile the queue at the next stop waiting for Bus 1 has become even longer, delaying Bus 1 even more, and enabling Bus 2 to get even closer. Soon the two buses are travelling together like one big bus. On a long bus route, Bus 3 will eventually begin to catch up as well. Which is why buses travel in threes.'

Who invented the ice lolly?

'It was all an accident. Back in 1923, on a very cold night, a lemonade salesman named Frank Epperson left a glass of lemonade with a spoon in it on a windowsill. The next morning the ice lolly was born.

On a football pitch, what's the point of the D-shaped area outside the penalty box?

It is there for one specific purpose: when a penalty is awarded, only the penalty taker and the goalkeeper are allowed to be in the penalty area. Every other player must be at least ten yards from the ball. The penalty area serves as an exclusion zone but it doesn't cover the area immediately behind the ball. Consequently, the 'D' or, as it is more properly known, 'the penalty arc', marks the area of the pitch that is ten yards from the penalty spot.

Why can't girls throw?

Can't they? Who says so?

Mitchell Symons in a book called, er, *Why Girls Can't Throw*.

Well, he's wrong. Oops, I mean, *I'm* wrong, for that writer is me.

There was a study done in the United States a few years ago in which 25 humans (none with any particular skill in throwing) and 17 monkeys were invited to throw balls into a bucket. The boys were 32 per cent more accurate than the girls when throwing with their chosen arm, but there was no difference

between them when they were all using their non-throwing arm. As for the monkeys, there was no difference at all between males and females.

It is thought that the reason the boys can throw better – or, to be precise, more accurately – than the girls is because parents teach their sons, rather than their daughters, how to throw. However, the study tested only accuracy. What about distance?

I decided to conduct a series of experiments to determine who could throw furthest. Over a six-month period I challenged (almost) every visitor to my house to come down to the beach and chuck stones or tennis balls as far as they could. This is what emerged:

1. Everyone threw further (and, indeed, straighter) with their better arm.

2. Where boys and girls were not

accustomed to throwing, the strongest threw the furthest. The strongest were usually the boys, but not always.

3. The person who threw the furthest was Kirsty, my bank manager, who is a girl, and an international lacrosse player.
4. I threw the shortest distance of anyone – including my wife.
5. When girls (of any age) threw, they treated it as a bit of a laugh, and giggled; when boys (of any age) threw, they took it very seriously indeed, and frowned.

Therefore we can conclude:

1. The ability to throw far depends on a combination of upper-body strength and technique.
2. The ability to throw accurately depends on technique.
3. Girls can be taught to throw as accurately as boys and (almost) as far.

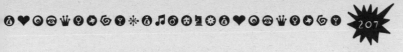

4. I am a complete girl.

5. Girls are superior human beings to boys.

So that's it. Girls *can* throw – except when they've never been shown how to, or when they decide to lob the ball in a giggly, girly fashion in order to reassure pathetic boys that they (the boys) are more powerful than them (the girls). But when girls are shown how to throw, and when they do it with the same intent, they can throw as accurately as any boy, and, where upper-body strength is equal, they can throw as far as any boy.

In my experiments, Kirsty was the only 'proper' sportsperson; however, it is an established fact that most professional male cricketers can throw further than most professional female cricketers.

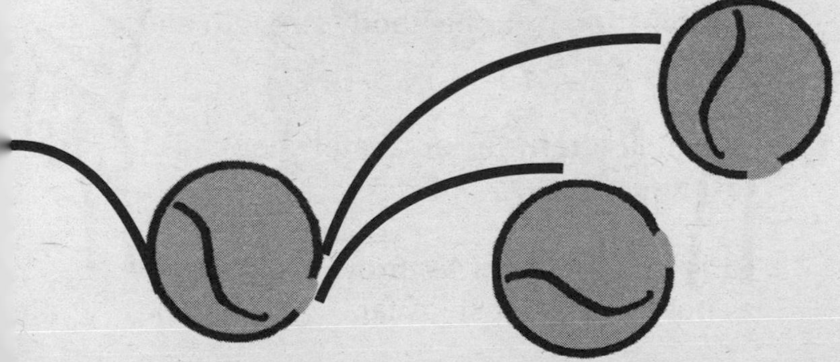

Why is it considered unlucky to whistle in a theatre?

It *is* unlucky – didn't you know?

Anyway, the taboo against whistling, especially backstage, comes from the pre-electricity era when a whistle was the signal for the curtains to close and the scenery to drop. An unexpected whistle could therefore cause an unexpected scene change, with all the problems you might imagine – such as furniture falling on the actors' heads!

Who was St Valentine?

In ancient Rome, 14 February was a holiday to honour Juno, the goddess of women and marriage. The following day was the beginning of the feast of Lupercalia, during which the names of Roman girls were written down on pieces of paper and put into jars. Roman boys would then pick girls at random and these couples would be together for the duration of the festival – with some of the couples staying together to get married.

I tell you this to illustrate the fact that, just like so many other days in the calendar (Easter and Christmas are obvious examples), St Valentine's Day has its roots in pre-Christian times.

But who was St Valentine?

He was a bishop of Terni, and he was martyred in Rome in around the year 270. His crime? Well, the Emperor Claudius II – known as Claudius the Cruel (remember, the clue is in the name) – was having great difficulty in persuading young men to join the army. He decided that this was because they didn't want to leave their wives and girlfriends, and so he banned marriages and engagements. Valentine, the bishop of Terni, was having none of it and continued to perform marriages in secret.

When he was discovered, he was condemned to be beaten to death with clubs and to have his head cut off on 14 February 270. Not a particularly nice way to go, but he was declared a martyr and then became a saint so I guess it turned out all right in the end. The point is, even if he had lived to be a hundred and died in his bed, he'd be dead by now anyway.

So now, thanks to him, every 14 February, otherwise perfectly sensible people send each other mushy cards, buy expensive flowers and place silly personal ads in newspapers. As for when this business of cards, etc., started, it is reckoned to be 1477, when one Margery Brews sent a letter to a man named John Paston addressed 'To my right welbelovyd Voluntyne'. This is believed to be the oldest Valentine's card.

However, according to legend, Valentine sent the first 'valentine' greeting himself. While in prison, he fell in love with a young girl – possibly the daughter of the prison warder – who visited him. Just before his death he wrote her a letter signed 'From your Valentine'. So there you have it. Or not, as the case may be.

Is it true that each of the four kings in a deck of playing cards represents a real king?

Yes, it is.

The King of Spades represents King David.

Clubs represents Alexander the Great.

Hearts represents Charlemagne.

Diamonds represents Julius Caesar.

Why are fat people jolly?

This book carries no author photograph, so you will have to take my word for it that the author is not the slimmest of men. In fact, it has been six years since he last saw his toes. When he walks down the street, he hears women muttering, 'Oh, that reminds me, I must buy some jelly for tonight's supper.' So if anyone is qualified to comment on the jolliness of fat people, it is he. Or, rather, me. However, I'm not particularly jolly, especially not when I'm reminded what a fatso I am.

Even so, I was keen to discover the origins of this myth. According to social anthropologists, fat people look like they take in so much of *everything* (food, drink, affection) that it is assumed they must be fun to be with. Personally, I am not convinced. I think it is much more likely that fat people try to be jolly so as to overcome thin people's prejudices. Plus, as people get older, the fat under their skin hides the stress lines that thin people can have, and so they look less haggard, and therefore jollier. But since I can't be sure, I'm going to go and eat a packet of Jaffa Cakes. Well, they've got fruit in them so they can't be bad for you.

Why do we tell people to 'sleep tight'?

This phrase originates from the days when mattresses were set upon ropes woven through the bed frame. Sagging ropes would, of course, have led to a poor night's sleep – hence the exhortation to 'sleep tight'. Incidentally, people would use bed keys to tighten sagging ropes.

Why is rugby sometimes called 'rugger'?

OK, there's football, right? But there are different kinds of football. So Rugby Football is, er, rugby, and Association Football is also known as 'soccer'. Apparently, in the late 19th century, public school and Oxbridge boys had a mania for putting -er on the ends of words as a form of slang. So just as breakfast became 'brekker', Association became 'soccer' – or, worse, 'footer' – and rugby 'rugger'.

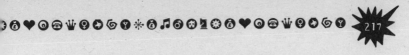

And, because these fellows controlled the sport for many years, it stuck.

Does the poo of a vegan smell less than the poo of a meat-eater?

I phoned the Vegan Society: 'Press one for information, two for membership, three for products, four for your nearest McDonald's.' OK, so I jest, but I hate those telephone menu thingies, and so I emailed their press officer – Tony Weston – and he wrote back.

'In my experience, sweaty vegans usually smell better than sweaty meat-eaters (dead food, rotting flesh and cheese takes its toll on your sweat glands). But poo . . . Now this really does depend on what's been eaten. Vegan food covers a wide spectrum of choices – these days you can get everything from vegan scampi and dairy-free chocolate ice cream to vegan caviar and champagne. Frutarians and raw-fooders are reputed to have very sweet-smelling poo. Vegans who eat a lot of vegetable curry have very spicy-smelling poo. The poos letting the side down are, I suspect, those resulting from the aftermath of lots of veggieburgers, vegan instant noodles and vegan bacon and sausages. The manufacturers now have flavourings so realistic that they not only taste great but have the same detrimental effect on the aroma of your poo. So, in summary, if your toilet has no extractor fan and you are looking for the ideal sweet-smelling lodger, better look for a vegan who eats a high proportion of raw fruit and vegetables.'

The Queen doesn't vote at elections, but do any other members of the royal family vote?

Even though Great Britain doesn't have a formal written constitution like they do in the United States, it has a constitution that has evolved over the years. This states that it is unconstitutional for the Queen to vote as she is expected to be impartial (that is to say, she shouldn't take sides).

Other members of the royal family, however, *are* allowed to vote – so long as they are not sitting members of the House of Lords. Interestingly, ever since the 1999 House of Lords Act, the princes and the dukes have no longer faced that restriction (because they are no longer allowed to sit in the House of Lords) but they still choose not to vote because they are as keen as the Queen is to promote the royal family's impartiality.

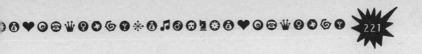

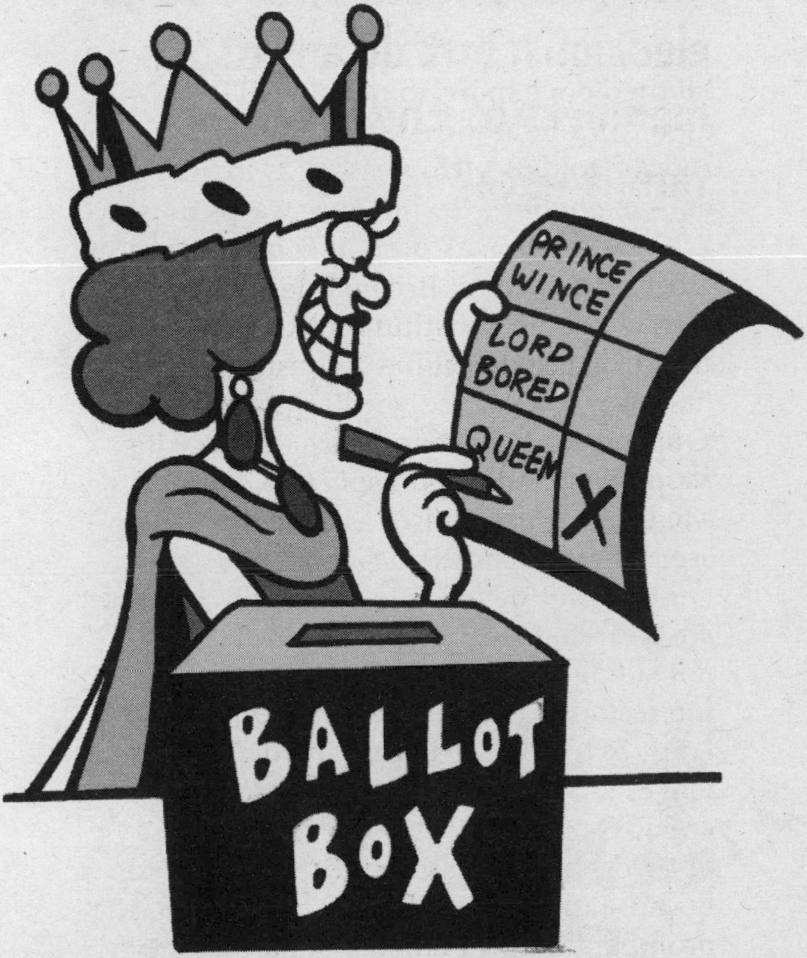
PRINCE WINCE
LORD BORED
QUEEN
X
BALLOT BOX

Wasps. Why?

I turned once more to my old pal Lucy, who used to work at the Natural History Museum, and she told me, 'Unpleasant as they might be' – *might* be? – 'to humans, wasps do serve a useful function as predators of flies and other insects.'

I'm still not convinced.

'OK, consider this then: there is a parasitic wasp that is used – and *sold* – to control whitefly in greenhouses as an alternative to using chemical pesticides.'

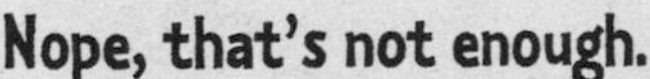

Nope, that's not enough.

'All right, what about the Kayapo Indians of the Amazon, who use wasps to protect their crops from leaf-cutting ants?'

Nah, it's still not enough to justify their existence – especially as I read that one person in 100 is potentially fatally allergic to wasp stings. I also learned that the best thing to do when threatened by a wasp is *not* to flap around and scream like a complete girly (my usual response). In fact, this behaviour can provoke an attack. Instead, gently raise your arms to protect your face and then stand still or move slowly away.

The other bad news is that getting stung once might not be the end of the experience. Wasp venom contains a chemical 'alarm pheromone' which, when released into the air, acts as a signal to other wasps to come and join in the stinging.

No, I really do think we could manage pretty well without them.

What is the origin of the expression, 'It's not over till the fat lady sings'?

I approached Dr Karen Landy, who said: 'If you are going to bother me with questions – for which, incidentally, I am not paid – you could at least phrase them correctly.'

Sorry.

'The expression is: "The opera ain't over till the fat lady sings", and it was first used by a sportswriter called Dan Cook in 1976 in the *San Antonio Express-News* to indicate that the sporting contest wouldn't end until time was called. In employing such a colourful metaphor, he was assuming that in every opera, a soprano – usually a large and curvaceous one – sings an aria at the end.

'The popularity of this expression spread when, a couple of years later, Cook started to use it in his broadcasts. During a playoff between the San Antonio Spurs and the Washington Bullets, the coach of the Washington Bullets overheard him and used the expression himself to caution fans against overconfidence. The phrase went on to become the team's rallying cry. From there, it entered the English language.'

Why doesn't Easter have a fixed date like Christmas does?

Originally Easter was celebrated on the same day as the Jewish Passover. Since the Jewish calendar is lunar, Passover can fall on any day of the week. The Church wanted to ensure that Easter would fall on a Sunday and so, after discussions that went on until the 8th century, the Church officially adopted the following formula: Easter Day is the first Sunday after the first full moon after the spring equinox (21 March). Thus, it can occur as early as 22 March and as late as 25 April (if the full moon after the equinox falls on a Sunday, Easter follows a week later).

However, Good Friday can never – repeat, *can never* – fall in December.

And why do I tell you this?

It's because one day some clever clogs will offer you a bet that Good Friday once fell on Boxing Day and you will know not to accept it. You see, this refers to a horse named Good Friday, which fell in a race held on 26 December 1899. So Good Friday fell on Boxing Day but not in the way you might have thought!

If someone's head is chopped off, does it retain any consciousness – even briefly?

After a lot of research – most of it rather gruesome – I have come to the conclusion that the answer is no. True, death by beheading might not be absolutely instantaneous. A severed head might for a split second have some reactions, which would account for the reported blinking eyes, or, in an experiment carried out on a guillotined criminal in 19th-century France, the reddened cheeks when the severed head is slapped. However, beheading is – as Dr Guillotine intended it to be – the most humane form of execution.

So, although you can find any number of gory stories about severed heads, that is all they are – stories, designed to shock and thrill you.

Why do we describe someone who is being obstructive as having a 'dog-in-the-manger' attitude?

The person who posed this question had obviously forgotten his *Aesop's Fables*. In the fable in question, there was a farm dog that

stopped the cattle from eating the grain in the manger even though he had no interest in eating it himself. The moral of the fable being: *People often begrudge others what they cannot enjoy themselves*. Hence the expression 'dog in the manger'.

If your eye came out of its socket but remained attached, could you turn it round and look at your own face?

How ghoulishly fascinating!

But it wasn't easy to find an answer.

First I phoned an ophthalmologist (eye doctor) from a leading chain of high-street opticians but he clearly thought I was mad and refused to answer my question. He wasn't the only one. Eventually, after talking to several 'experts' (definition of an expert: one who has made every mistake possible in a single field), I got hold of one who – disappointingly – told me, 'Typically, if your eye came out it would be so damaged you probably wouldn't be able to see *anything* out of it – let alone look at your own face.'

Why's that?

In a bored I-can't-believe-I'm-talking-to-this-moron voice, he explained, 'Any trauma that could cause an eye to come out of its socket would make it so bad that it would cease to work.'

So that, I'm afraid, is that. Pity really.

Has anyone in a film ever played mother or father to someone who, in real life, was older than them?

Back in 1940s and 1950s Hollywood, middle-aged male stars carried on playing young men well into their fifties, while female stars would be put out to grass (i.e. restricted to character roles) as soon as they reached 35. As a result, it isn't so remarkable to find actresses playing (male) stars' mothers when they weren't much older than them. However, the only example I could find of a 'mother' younger than her 'son' was when the actress Jessie Royce Landis, 54, played the mother of Cary Grant, 55, in the Hitchcock classic, *North by Northwest* (1959).

Even more extraordinary than that was the casting of Lionel Jeffries, 42, as the father of Dick Van Dyke, 43, in the 1968 film *Chitty Chitty Bang Bang*.

What's the origin of the expression 'by hook or by crook'?

This one goes all the way back to medieval times, when people – desperate for wood to use as fuel – were allowed to take branches and twigs that had fallen from trees on land owned by the Crown, although they were not allowed on the land itself. These people weren't stupid and so, if they were farmers and had reapers (which looked like hooks), or if they were shepherds and had crooks, they'd do their utmost to get as much wood as possible by any means at their disposal – or, in other words, by hook or by crook.

Are there any sports in which women compete on equal terms with men?

Yes, there are sports where women compete on equal terms, especially those involving equipment that is more important than, or just as important as, the person. For example, the horse in equestrian events, the car in motor sport, the boat in sailing.

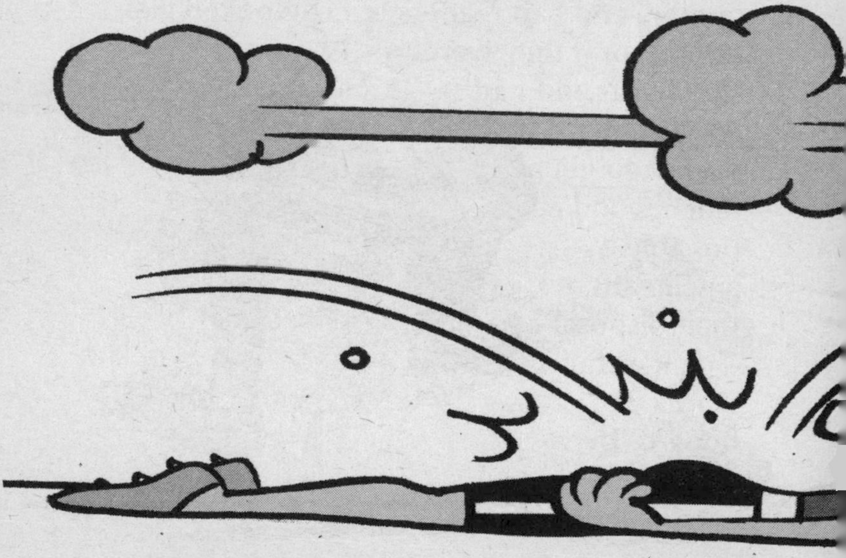

Although women can't acquire the same upper-body strength as their male counterparts, they can do just as well – if not better – in extreme endurance sports such as long-distance running and long-distance swimming.

As an 'international language', why isn't Esperanto used at the United Nations?

Esperanto was invented in 1887 by a Pole named Dr Zamenhof and he called it Esperanto because it means 'the one who hopes'. Unfortunately, hope is all that was achieved. Hardly anyone speaks this artificial language, which is a combination of French, Italian, Spanish and English. Indeed, in the US there are more people who speak Klingon, a language made up by/for fans of *Star Trek*, than there are Esperanto speakers.

Is it possible for hair to turn white overnight?

This is a bit of an urban myth. There is a story that Marie Antoinette's hair turned white the night before her execution. But this is impossible, because white hair would have to grow through from the roots and that would take weeks.

However, there might be an explanation. If someone has a mixture of, say, black and white hair, and if, due to stress, they suffer from sudden and severe hair loss, then they might lose their black hair. This would leave them with just their white hair – thereby giving the impression that all their hair had suddenly turned white.

What is a Community Chest – as found in a game of Monopoly?

In America, where the game originated, a Community Chest is – or, rather, was – a group of local charities which joined together for fund-raising. Nowadays it's known as the United Way.

Which sport is the most dangerous for its spectators?

I asked a few sports journalists this question. Someone suggested it was cricket, because you die of boredom . . .

Although no one knew for sure, they were able to make educated guesses. For a start, there was some agreement on the most dangerous sports for participants (yes, I know that's not the question): BASE jumping, free diving, speed skiing (the world's fastest non-motorized sport), bull riding and solo yacht racing were all named – and there was a special mention for people who ride bicycles during the rush hour.

The most dangerous sport for spectators is much harder to decide on. Motor racing is an obvious candidate. In 1955, for example, a Mercedes left the track at Le Mans and killed 80 spectators, but there are now so many safety features in motor racing that deaths are a rarity, whether of participants or of spectators.

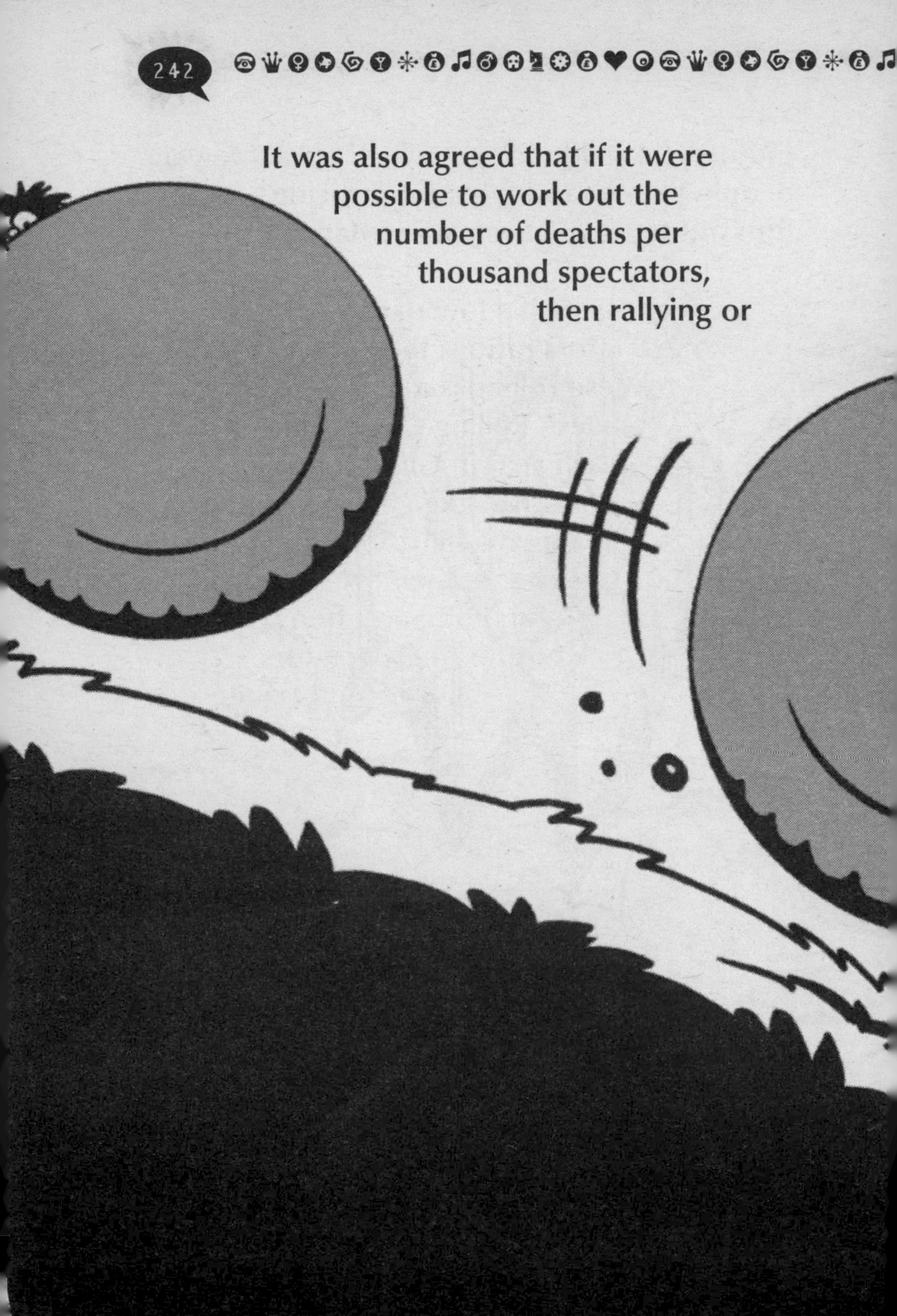

It was also agreed that if it were possible to work out the number of deaths per thousand spectators, then rallying or motorcycle road racing – which attract fewer people than Grand Prix motor racing – might turn out to be *relatively* more dangerous.

Then again, if a low participants-to-spectators ratio is the criterion, then cheese rolling is a possibility. The Cheese Rolling Competition held each year in Gloucester sees massive 4 kg cheeses hurled down a hill and chased. The cheeses achieve speeds of 40 mph and often crash into the spectators – injuring them quite badly.

Why were unmarried women called spinsters?

Up until the 18th century, unmarried women who had nowhere else to go were often sent to 'spin houses' – a type of workhouse – to spin yarn. As a result, they were known as 'spinsters', and eventually this came to be the term by which all unmarried women were known. Now very few people use the word.

Why do we say that someone is the 'spitting image' of someone else?

Like so many phrases that have worked their way into our language, this is a result of a mispronunciation of a perfectly simple phrase. In the southern states of America it used to be said of a boy who looked and behaved like his father that he was the 'spirit and image' of him. It's not hard to see how 'spirit and image' could evolve into 'spitting image'.

Before the fruit was discovered, how was the colour 'orange' referred to?

Gold, amber, yellow, red, tawny . . . and all points in between (e.g. yellowish-red, light amber, deep tawny, etc.). The English language has never been short of words.

However, until we had the fruit there wasn't much around in the colour orange. The

important thing to know is that the fruit came *before* the colour and not the other way round. The fruit was brought to Spain from south-east Asia by Arab traders around the 9th century and was given the Arabic name *naranj* – after the Sanskrit word for 'orange tree' (*naranga*). By the time the fruit came to England, we called it 'naranja' and then 'norange'. Eventually the letter 'n' was dropped from the beginning – 'an orange' and 'a norange' being identical in speech. Although the fruit first turned up here in the 14th century, the first record we have of the colour is in 1620.

Why is the sea blue?

Do you want the difficult or the (relatively) simple explanation?

Yup, I thought so. Here goes then.

If you take a bucket of seawater, it is, of course, colourless. So how come it looks blue when there's lots of it? Well, obviously, there's the matter of the blue sky being reflected in the sea, but it's got much more to do with the sun's rays. The water absorbs all the sun's rays beating down on it. However, the redder colours in the spectrum get absorbed better than the bluer colours, and so you tend to get left with a combination of those blue colours (blue, indigo and violet), which changes according to the position of you and of the sun, and also according to the sun's intensity.

Where did the word 'bonfire' come from?

This is pretty grisly so you might not want to read any further.

Oh well – you can't say I didn't warn you!

In the 16th century a popular method of execution (though not popular, you can be sure, with the poor souls on whom it was inflicted) was burning at the stake. In the words of the day, this was described as – and I did warn you that this would be horrible – a 'bone fire'. The two words came together to become one: bonfire. And we still use the word, although we are no longer burning bones in the fire.

Why do some people have fair hair as children but dark hair as adults?

You need only one of your parents, grandparents or even great-grandparents to be blond for it to be possible for you to be blond as a small child. However, as you get older, your hair darkens unless the genes for being blond are very strong – which means that more of your ancestors have to have been blond.

So, if all 14 parents, grandparents and great-grandparents were blond, then the child will be blond for all of his or her life. But the fewer blond ancestors, the less likely it is that the child will remain blond as he or she grows older.

Why do we call someone who misbehaves a 'hooligan'?

This is all down to a 19th-century Irishman named Patrick Hooligan, who was notorious for fighting – especially in bars. He was also incredibly strong. He could lift four large men onto his back and then stagger with

them across the bar-room floor. After a while his reputation for fighting spread so far that bars – even bars he had never visited – put up signs saying that Hooligan wouldn't be served. Eventually, his name became an eponym – that is to say that any brawling man would be called a hooligan.

Why is the scoring system 15, 30, 40 used in tennis?

It comes from the clock. The first point is quarter past (or 15), the second is half past (or 30) and the 40 was originally 45 (or three-quarters) but got shortened. The word 'love' – for zero – comes from the French word *l'oeuf*, meaning 'egg', which, of course, resembles a zero. As for 'deuce', which is what 40–40 is called, this comes from the French *deux* because it takes two consecutive points to win the game.

Why are we said to 'tie the knot' when we get married?

Research suggests there are three possible explanations:

1. The Carthaginians (from an ancient city in northern Africa) used to tie the thumbs of the bride and bridegroom together with a leather lace.

2. In ancient Rome brides wore girdles that were tied in knots which the groom had to untie.

3. In the Hindu marriage ceremony the groom has to tie a ribbon around the bride's neck.

Any one of those – or, indeed, all three of them – will do for me.

Why are important days often known as 'red-letter days'?

This goes back to the early church almanacs, when religious festivals and saints' days would be printed in red ink. Modern diaries and calendars maintained this tradition of distinguishing special days with the colour red, and so nowadays any significant day – even if it is significant only to an individual (such as their birthday) – is described as a red-letter day.

Who was 'Mary, Mary, Quite Contrary' in the nursery rhyme?

Mary, Mary, quite contrary
How does your garden grow?
With silver bells and cockleshells
And pretty maids all in a row.

There are quite a few possibilities, but the most likely is that the poem referred to Mary, Queen of Scots (1542–1587). 'How does your garden grow?' would have been a reference to how she was ruling the country. The 'silver bells' represented the Catholic cathedral bells, and the 'pretty maids' were the ladies of her court who were more beautiful than her.

How did the Canary Islands get their name?

The Canary Islands (which include Gran Canaria, Tenerife and Lanzarote) are not – as you might have thought – named after the canary bird. In fact, they were named after dogs. When the ancient Romans first arrived on Gran Canaria, they were struck by the large, scary dogs they found there, and so they called the place *Insularia Canaria* (the Island of Dogs).

Over time, this became 'Canary Island', and was eventually used to cover all the islands in the group.

As for the bird, it is native to the Canary Islands and the surrounding regions, and that's how it got its name, not the other way round.

How did mayonnaise get its name?

In 1756 the Duke of Richelieu led the French forces to victory over the English at Port Mahon. To celebrate, the duke's chef prepared a huge banquet. On the menu was a sauce made from cream and eggs. When the chef realized, to his horror, that there was no cream in the kitchen, he improvised, and substituted olive oil for the cream.

A new culinary masterpiece was born, and the chef named it *Mahonnaise* in honour of the duke's victory at Port Mahon. It soon became widely known as mayonnaise.

Why does a bridegroom have a best man?

To hold his hand and make a speech, I'd have thought – oh, and to make sure he turns up in the first place.

However, it turns out that the best man's role was once very different. In northern Europe in the 5th century, men didn't so much propose to women as drag them off and force them to get married. The best man's job was to prevent the bride's family from stopping the wedding. That's why, even today, the best man and the groom both stand to the right of the bride – just in case they need to draw their swords . . .

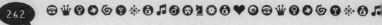

If Edward VIII hadn't given up the throne, but had died childless, who would be monarch today?

In this hypothetical situation, let's say that Edward ruled from 1936 until his death in 1972. He would then have been succeeded by the next oldest of his brothers. If the next oldest brother was no longer alive, Edward would have been succeeded by that brother's oldest boy child, or, if there were no sons, that brother's oldest daughter. In other words, King Edward would have been succeeded by the oldest child of his next oldest brother, Albert (who in fact became King George VI) – namely by Princess Elizabeth, our current Queen; the only difference being that she would have taken the throne in 1972, instead of in 1952.

The way it goes is that the moment the eldest son produces an heir, that heir supersedes the father's younger brothers. For example, the Queen produced four children. Before they had any children themselves, Prince Charles was heir to the throne, followed by Prince Andrew, Prince Edward and Princess Anne. The moment Prince William was born, he leapfrogged Andrew, Edward and Anne in the line of succession. Similarly, Andrew's daughters take precedence over Edward and Anne.

Why are people who show their feelings said to 'wear their hearts on their sleeves'?

In the Middle Ages, on 14 February, it was the custom for young men and women to pick names out of a bowl to see who their Valentines would be for the next week. The practice was for them to wear these names (inscribed on heart-shaped pieces of paper or fabric) on their sleeves for a whole week. Therefore, wearing your heart on your sleeve became a way of saying that you had made your feelings obvious.

Fred
x
Lil

Who first thought of kissing the Blarney Stone?

The Blarney Stone is a block of limestone that was built into the battlements of Blarney Castle, near Cork in Ireland. According to legend, whoever kisses the stone will be granted the gift of the gab and become a great speaker.

But where did this legend arise?

Way back in 1602, Cormac MacCarthy, the Lord of Blarney and the owner of Blarney Castle, was able to fend off representatives of Queen Elizabeth I, who were trying to gain ownership of his land. He was so clever that he was able to do this purely by talking them out of it.

What might have helped him was the Blarney Stone, built into his castle. This block of stone was believed to be half of the Stone of Scone, given by Robert the Bruce to one of MacCarthy's ancestors in recompense for his help in the Battle of Bannockburn (1314), and it was said to have magical qualities.

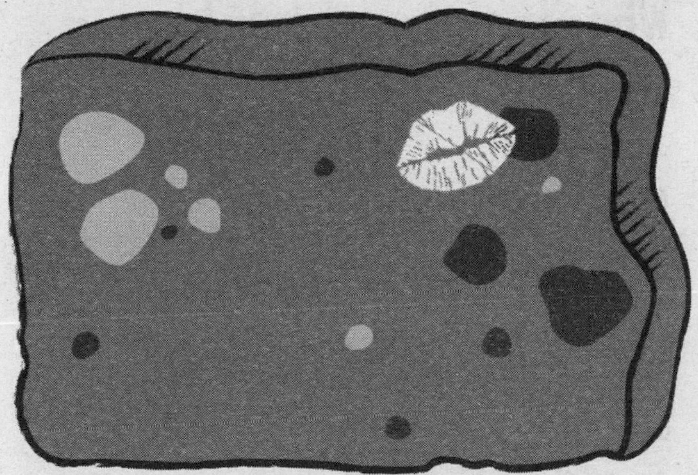

From there grew the legend that anyone who kissed the stone would be a fluent and persuasive speaker.

It should be said, however, that locals are less impressed and – or so it's said – even wee on the stone at night when no one's looking!

Why are detectives known as 'private eyes'?

In 1925 the American Pinkerton Agency – probably the most famous private detective agency in the world – ran an advertising campaign that featured a large picture of an eye and the slogan, 'We never sleep'. As a direct result of this advertising, private detectives became known as private eyes.

Do dock leaves really lessen the pain of nettle stings?

We all know that dock leaves grow next to stinging nettles, but is it true that they soothe the sting, or is it just in the mind?

While it's true that there is a benefit in having (almost) anything rubbed on your legs after you've been stung, there is scientific evidence that dock leaves have a proper therapeutic effect. Put simply: nettle stings contain histamines, which cause swelling, while the juice of dock leaves contains antihistamines, which reduce it. To get the full benefit, you should crush the dock leaf to release its juice.

Isn't nature wonderful?

Why don't people ride zebras?

Just because it looks like a horse doesn't mean it is one! Although there have been occasional instances of zebras being ridden for a few minutes, or put in harness and used alongside ponies to draw a carriage, they are basically unrideable.

Why?

Because, unlike horses, zebras are nasty, stubborn animals that have no desire whatsoever to have humans perched on their backs. To be fair to them, this might not be solely because of their faulty temperament. It could be because they are relatively weak and wouldn't survive carrying a heavy load in this way.

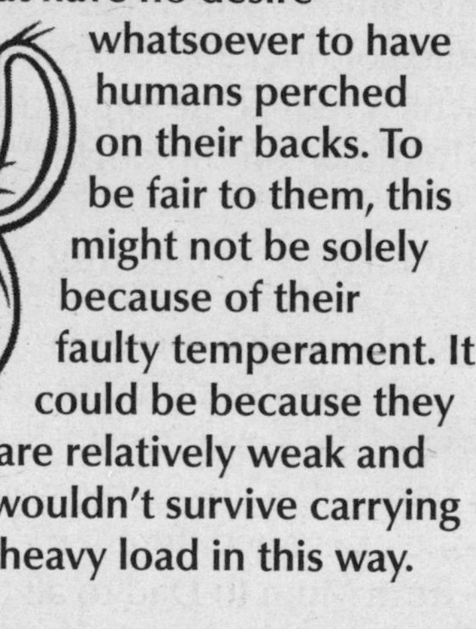

How do parrots learn to imitate human speech?

Parrots learn to talk just like humans: by imitating sounds. However, humans also learn the meaning of words, but parrots never do – they simply repeat them, er, parrot fashion.

But it's extraordinary enough that they can reproduce the sounds – even if they don't know what they're saying. How is this possible?

Unlike humans, parrots don't have vocal cords, but they can control the movement of the muscles in their throat in a way that enables them to copy certain sounds – including human speech (as most other birds can't).

Some parrots – especially African Greys – are superb mimics and can reproduce not only words but also different accents (even from within the same family). Someone I know had a parrot that could say 'walkies' in the same tone as every different member of a family – from Mum to Dad to all the three children. The family dog used to go berserk!

Why do our teeth chatter when we're cold?

Our bodies are designed to function at around 37°C. If we're colder than that, our muscles try to warm us up by moving involuntarily. These muscles include the ones that control our teeth – and that explains why they chatter.

Why do we give people the 'brush off'?

In times gone by, hotel porters would look after guests by making sure that they looked immaculate just before they set out for the evening. They did this by running a brush over a gentleman's clothing. Gentlemen who were known to tip badly didn't get much of a brushing down; instead, they got just a few strokes of the brush or, in other words (and here we come to the origin of the expression), the 'brush off'.

SMALL TIP
BIG TIP

What is the meaning of life?

Let me start by telling you a story. There was once a village whose inhabitants decided they had to know the meaning of life. They went to the wise man who lived in a cave (not so wise, you might think, but that's the way it was). He told them to bring him all their money and he would let them know the answer. So they went away, returned with everything they had, and waited.

'The meaning of life,' said the wise man, 'is a lemon.'

After they'd recovered from the shock, they were angry. 'What are you saying, wise man? We have given you all our money to discover the meaning of life, and you tell us that it's a lemon?'

The wise man looked at them and shrugged. 'All right then, it's not a lemon.'

What else? Well, Douglas Adams, who wrote *The Hitchhiker's Guide to the Galaxy*, told us that 42 is the answer to everything but I don't know if that includes life. Stumped for any other possibilities, I decided to ask my wiser friends what they thought. The most profound response was: 'It is the question. "What is the meaning of life?" is itself the meaning of life – the process of enquiring about life.'

But I think my favourite answer came from my friend Tim. He said, 'For me, the meaning of life is like a set of keys that has gone missing. The more you fret about them, the further away you are from finding them. The chances are you'll only find them when you stop looking.'

Interesting. It is also probable that they will be in the last place you would consider looking. In other words, you have to think outside the box.

Still not satisfied? OK. Victorian writer Samuel Butler said that 'life is one long process of getting tired', and John Lennon declared that 'life is what happens to you while you're busy making other plans', while the American philosopher George Santayana concluded 'there is no cure for birth and death save to enjoy the interval'.

Why are old people described as being 'long in the tooth'?

Funnily enough, although this expression is almost exclusively used about people, it was originally applied to animals – specifically horses.

As horses get older, their gums recede – so although their teeth are not getting longer, they appear to be. Therefore the more tooth that's visible (because of gum shrinkage), the older the horse is. Hence 'long in the tooth'.

Incidentally, another expression arises from this. Since a horse's teeth (or, to be more accurate, gums) are an indication of its age, one might check it out by looking in its mouth. But someone being given a *free* horse really has no right to start quibbling about how old it is. From here we get the saying, 'never look a gift horse in the mouth'.

Why do people slump in front of the telly all night?

According to social anthropologist Dr Lorraine Mackintosh, 'It could well be a throwback to the days when a caveman returned from an unsuccessful day's hunting. He would sit and gaze at the horizon for hours for any sign of animals. Fast-forward several thousand years and when his descendants get home from an unsuccessful day at school or at work, instead of gazing at the horizon, they gaze at the TV.'

What is the origin of the phrase 'saved by the bell'? Is it anything to do with the end of a lesson at school?

No, it isn't! This goes back hundreds of years to a time when medical facilities were unheard of and it wasn't always possible to tell if someone was definitely dead. Coffins opened years later were sometimes found to have scratches on their lids. On their *inside* lids . . . Creepy. So people insisted on being buried with bells so they could ring them if it turned out they'd been merely unconscious, rather than dead. Hence the expression 'dead ringer'.

But who would hear such a noise?

The man who was paid to sit near the grave for the night and listen for the sound of a bell would be working 'the graveyard shift'. And if he heard the tinkling sound, then the person inside the coffin would indeed have been saved by the bell.

RING!
HELLO
RING!
HELLO!
Z Z Z
Z Z Z

Has anyone ever lived under the sea?

In 1969 the American government launched the Tektite Project, which was designed to investigate the effects on human beings of living and working underwater for extended periods of time.

An underwater world was placed on concrete footings some 20 metres below the surface of Beehive Cove, on the Caribbean island of St John's. It consisted of two towers joined together by a passageway. Inside the towers were four circular rooms, plus another room that served as a galley (kitchen), engine room and laboratory. More importantly, there was also a wet room with a hatch in the floor through which divers could enter and leave the habitat.

The four men who lived there were dubbed 'aquanauts' and they had plenty of luxuries, including television (phew!). The aquanauts were monitored for the record 58 days they spent underwater and they emerged in reasonable health.

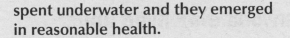

In 1986 one of the people involved in the Tektite Project, Ian Koblick, created Jules' Undersea Lodge, the world's only undersea hotel in Key Largo, Florida. Here ordinary people (i.e. non-aquanauts and non-scientists) could have a taste of life under the sea.

Where is the most well-trodden square metre of land on the planet?

I would have thought it was one of the world's most popular tourist sites – like Madame Tussaud's – but the ground outside places like that isn't trodden on when they aren't open.

Religious places – like the Sacred Mosque of Mecca, and Lourdes – are also extremely busy, but some of this is seasonal.

No, for day-in, day-out heavy usage you would have to go to the pedestrian crossing outside Tokyo's Shinjuku railway station, which is apparently walked on by a million people every day of the year.

Do identical twins have identical fingerprints?

No. Although identical twins share genes and DNA, they don't have identical fingerprints. That's because fingerprints aren't genetic. They form randomly while we're in the womb and develop as we grow.

Why do the nouns in some languages, such as French and Spanish, have genders?

You know when you're on a long car journey and your kid sister or brother is asking your mum and dad lots of difficult questions ('Where does the white go when the snow melts?'), and eventually someone – usually the driver – snaps, 'Because it *does*, all right?'

Well, this is one of those questions. And the answer's the same: because they do, all right?

I could try telling you that as languages developed – and they do just that: develop – certain words come to take on male or female characteristics, but there are so many exceptions to the various 'rules' linguists have tried to establish over the years that the answer 'because they do' is probably the best.

la bouteille

le verre

What's the difference between a model, a top model and a supermodel?

What indeed! Once upon a time – and I know you'll find this hard to believe – all models were anonymous. The people who read fashion magazines were only interested in the clothes the models were wearing. Occasionally, if a particular model married a very rich man, then her name might be mentioned in the newspaper, but otherwise they weren't at all famous.

Then came the 1960s, and models like Jean Shrimpton and Twiggy caught the public imagination. They were dubbed – not unreasonably – 'top models' because they were, er, top models.

Fast-forward now to the 1980s and 1990s and the rise to fame of Claudia Schiffer, Cindy Crawford, Kate Moss, Naomi Campbell and Linda Evangelista. They were all top models, to be sure, but in that era of hype, that wasn't enough. So they were branded 'supermodels'.

The result of this is that nowadays every model seems to be a supermodel. That's word inflation for you.

Why does asparagus make your wee smell?

If you've ever eaten asparagus, you must have noticed. Or maybe you haven't? According to the chemist I spoke to – and I must admit I only understood about one word in three – only some of us have the (un)necessary gene that makes our urine smell after eating asparagus. What happens is that there's a sulphurous compound found in foods like asparagus and garlic, which, when broken down by our digestive systems, comes out in our wee a little later. And it smells rank.

Is it true that, given an infinite amount of time, a chimpanzee with a typewriter could produce the complete works of Shakespeare?

However long infinity is, it is not long enough for a chimp to press enough random typewriter keys to churn out Shakespeare's entire output. Let me illustrate this:

rofjfkjgutjjnfjj%yyghEythytuyrr
uFdsrejdf'poiyhry\hrtyyhyl;sk`d
f'pohgrv85ghfh4ht00-95mbklj-
9084upo23082iu4cfmbnv[905]-06=6-
0y';uiewiwepoiwripertupy-0yjhgyouryooy
[trw045jirut uuu8488557jjfehrkso][yyrEh0
y';uiewiwepoiwripertupy-0yjhgyouryooy[t
rw045jirut mnvhg6urhi00606886868ufgl\

Yes, that's what I got from approaching this task in the same way as a chimp would, and it doesn't bear much resemblance to 'To be

or not to be, that is the question' (even if you leave out the spacing). Given that there are 26 letters in the alphabet – and assuming a typewriter that doesn't have any punctuation marks on it – the chances of producing that tiny phrase would be one in 26 to the power of 30 (that's ignoring spaces as well as punctuation), and it's a figure much too large for my calculator to work out. The odds against that are so huge that it is safe to say that it wouldn't happen from, well, here to infinity – and beyond. As for the complete works . . .

Why do we say that someone who is spouting rubbish is talking gobbledygook?

It's not often that you can pinpoint the first time a word or phrase was used, but this is an exception. On 30 March 1944 a man named Maury Maverick, a congressman who was serving as chairman of the United States Smaller War Plants Corporation, wrote a memo to staff banning what he called 'gobbledygook language'. He went on to threaten that 'anyone using the words *activation* or *implementation* will be shot'. Later, when the word began to be used by other people, Maverick explained that the word was based on the turkey, which was 'always gobbledy gobbling and strutting with ludicrous pomposity. At the end of his gobble, there was a sort of gook.'

GOBBLEDYGOOK

Is it morally wrong to copy a CD you buy for a friend's birthday before you give it to them?

This is, in fact, an extremely complex conundrum. My own view is that, provided the CD is in no way damaged by the copying and the recipient is not informed, it is perfectly proper. However, I was keen to discuss the issue further with experts. But who? In the end I settled for an acquaintance and two friends. The acquaintance was Father Michael (a Catholic priest). The friends were Stuart, who has a degree in philosophy, and Steve, a professional songwriter.

Father Michael's view was that it was only justifiable if you told the recipient what you had done – that you were honest.

Stuart was opposed to it, on the basis that the moment you copied the CD – whether you told your friend or not – it ceased to be a gift. 'That is to say, by your very actions you alter the quality of the object.'

I expected Steve, who stands to lose money in royalties every time a CD is copied, to be opposed, but he was all for it. It didn't help that he misunderstood me at first and thought I was offering to copy something for him. 'Nah,' he said, 'it's cool. For every person who copies a CD, there are a dozen who will buy it, and the more people who hear something, the better it is for all of us – even if it is illegal.'

Why do we call an inquisitive person a 'nosy parker'?

We get the expression 'nosy parker' from Matthew Parker, who was Archbishop of Canterbury in the 16th century. He had a very long nose and was extremely inquisitive – hence Nosy Parker.

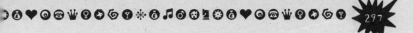

Did any Japanese kamikaze pilots survive the war?

I contacted historian Dr Michael Morgan, who told me that the answer was yes.

'As most people know, the role of the kamikaze – "divine wind" – pilots was to fly rudimentary planes packed with explosives straight into Allied ships in what was really a suicide mission. However, to complete their task, they had to find an Allied ship, and if they couldn't they returned to base. There was one kamikaze pilot who flew no fewer than *11* missions and lived through the entire war.'

Do blind people 'see' in their dreams?

Interesting question, and for the answer I turned to Ron, a family friend who has been blind since he was four years old.

'Because I had sight – if only for a few years – I do sometimes see images in my dreams but it's not really seeing as you or any other sighted person would understand it. I feel more than see in my dreams: I sense things as all the events of the past day, week, month get jumbled around in my mind.

'Friends of mine who've never had any sight tell me that they don't see anything in their dreams because "seeing" is something they simply don't do, but the other senses are magnified to compensate for it. More to the point, although all of us – blind and sighted – dream, many people simply forget their dreams as soon as they wake up.

'The people I envy – although I'm not the envious kind – are the very few who are lucky enough not only to have visual dreams but also to dream in colour. How wonderful must that be!'

What's the origin of the expression 'the whole nine yards'?

This comes from the Second World War, when US fighter planes in the South Pacific were equipped with machine-gun ammunition belts; stretched out on the ground, these measured precisely 27 feet. (There are three feet in one yard, so 27 feet is the equivalent of nine yards.)

So, if a pilot fired all his ammo at a target, he was said to have gone 'the whole nine yards'.

Do hair and nails continue to grow on a corpse after death?

Ooh, it's a spooky thought, isn't it? A person is dead and yet their body is still alive! Maybe they are still feeling sensations even though their brains have stopped functioning? And if their hair can keep growing, perhaps other parts can regenerate themselves. *Are we talking about the living dead?!!*

Calm down. It's all a lot less worrying than that. I talked to Dr James Peters, a part-time pathologist, about it.

'When someone dies, that's it: finito,' he said. 'They are dead. Everything stops. The blood stops flowing and so the hair and nails stop growing.'

So why this rumour about hair and nails continuing to grow?

'What happens is that the body dries out after death and so the skin on the scalp –

and, for that matter, around the fingernails – recedes a little, which might give the impression that the hair and the nails have grown. But they haven't.'

Is it dangerous to suppress a fart?

I turned to Dr Roland Powell and he was absolutely insistent that it *isn't* dangerous to suppress a fart. 'On the contrary,' he said with his usual smile, 'it might be dangerous to fart in certain circumstances.'

Such as?

'Use your imagination.'

Is that it?

'Well, I can explain why it is that this myth came about. It is, after all, an unpleasant sensation to hold onto wind, but it is utterly harmless. No one ever ruptured themselves by holding back a fart.'

'So how do farts work?

All right. It's all to do with the air and gases – including methane – that you take into your intestines. Belches, which come from the stomach, consist mostly of air but farts are produced by bacteria working on undigested food in the colon. Now, some foods – such as baked beans – can't be broken down by the body's digestive juices and so, as they ferment in your colon, they cause wind. But it's not just baked beans: different people are unable to digest different foods – for example, dairy products – and will react accordingly when they eat them.'

And why do farts smell?

'Basically because of where they originate.'

We know that when you flush a toilet in the southern hemisphere, the water swirls the opposite way to the northern hemisphere. If my toilet was on the equator – half in the northern hemisphere and half in the south – would it explode all over me?

Well, first I flew straight to Australia to check out the question, and it turns out that although bathwater does swirl the opposite way down a plughole in the southern hemisphere, toilet water *doesn't*.

Even if toilet water did flush the other way – and it didn't, trust me – then what do you think would happen on the equator? Obviously, it would just go down straight – not clockwise or counter-clockwise, but straight down. Rather like the sun sets immediately on the equator but takes longer the further north (where summer is in June, July and August) and the further south (where summer is in December, January and February) you go.

Questions I wasn't able to answer

How come wrong numbers are never engaged?

When cheese gets its picture taken, what does it say?

How do you throw away a dustbin?

If a vegetarian eats vegetables, what does a humanitarian eat?

What is a free gift? Aren't all gifts free?

If you try to fail, and succeed, which have you done?

Why isn't there mouse-flavoured cat food?

Why do cream crackers split into three whenever you try to butter them?

If, according to the proverb, a fool and his money are soon parted, how did they get together in the first place?

Why can't you buy a tube of toothpaste without an extra 10 per cent free?

If corn oil is made from corn, what is baby oil made from?

How come there are 365 days in the year when a year consists of 52 weeks of seven days each?

Why are they called 'stairs' inside but 'steps' outside?